Sociopolitics

Essay Series 18

Paris Arnopoulos

Sociopolitics
Political Development
in Postmodern Societies

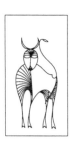

Guernica
Toronto / New York
1995

Antonio D'Alfonso, editor
Guernica Editions Inc.
P.O. Box 117, Station P, Toronto (Ontario), Canada M5S 2S6
340 Nagel Drive, Cheektowaga, N.Y. 14225-4731, USA

Printed in Canada.

The Publisher gratefully acknowledges support from
The Canada Council and Ontario Arts Council.

Legal Deposit – Second Quarter
National Library of Canada.

Library of Congress Catalog Card Number: 94-78581

Canadian Cataloguing in Publication Data

Arnopoulos, Paris
Sociopolitics : political development in postmodern societies

(Essay series ; 18)
Includes bibliographical references.
ISBN 0-920717-99-3

1 . Political sociology.
I . Title. II . Series: Essay series (Toronto, Ont.) ; 18.
JA76 . A74 1994   306 . 2   C94-900646-7

Table of Contents

Foreword   7

INTRODUCTION   9

PART ONE: INFOSOCIETY

I.   CYBERPOLITICS
     System Model of Science, Technology and Society   15

II. INFOPOLITICS
     Political Power in Infosociety   31

PART TWO: ECOSOCIETY

III. ECOPOLITICS
     Societies in the Postindustrial Era   77

IV. GAIAPOLITICS
     The Ecosociety in a Turbulent World   145

PART THREE: TECHNOSOCIETY

V.   TECHNOPOLITICS
     Telecommunitary Democracy   213

VI. METAPOLITICS
     Defining Political Development   257

Conclusion   289

Analytic Index   293

Thematic Bibliography   301

For Kathy

Foreword

The contents of this book were originally written as five separate consultative reports to various national and international organizations.

The First Chapter began as a report on the social impact of Science and Technology, and was written for the Information Society Program of the GAMMA Institute of Montreal.

The Infopolitics Chapter, originally Politics in the Information Society, was written for the Ministry of State for Science and Technology of the Canadian Government in Ottawa.

The Ecopolitics and Gaiapolitics Chapters, originally The Political Aspects of the Conserver Society Project, were written for the Privy Council Office of the Canadian Government in Ottawa.

The Technopolitics Chapter, originally the Telecommunitary Democracy Report, was written for the New International Information Order Program of the United Nations Educational, Scientific and Cultural Organization in Paris.

Finally, the last Chapter was a Political Development Essay written for the Goals, Processes and Indicators of Development Program of the United Nations University in Tokyo.

These five essays were done at various times in the past fifteen years. They have been completely revised now for their first publication together as the six chapters of this book. Because of their general and theoretical nature their essential content is perennial, so they are as pertinent today as they were then. It is for that reason that they have been reissued at this critical time for more academic and wider public distribution.

P. J. Arnopoulos
January 1993

Introduction

This book is about the evolution of politics in advanced social systems. We have termed this phenomenon *Sociopolitics*, defined as the public affairs of postmodern society. This particular type of politics is presently emerging in the developed world and may be the vanguard of the social order in the next century.

After two centuries of industrialism, the mature societies of Western Europe, North America and Pacific Oceania are showing distinct signs of transition to a new era of what might be called *postmodernism*. Generated by the high technology of informediation and telecommunication, the new era is changing not only the economics of production, but the culture of consumption and, last but not least, the politics of participation.

As the Industrial Revolution introduced mechanical energy and mass production which ended ten millennia of the agricultural era, so the Technological Revolution introduces artificial intelligence and genetic engineering which is now changing the face of the Earth at the dawn of the third millennium. After the Agricultural and Industrial, the Technological Revolution is the third wave of macrohistory which ushers in the postindustrial economy and along with it the postmodern society.

Of course, the whole world is not moving in step. Most regions are still struggling to pull out of the agricultural period. For two-thirds of humanity, mostly in the Third World of Africa, Asia and Latin America, the primary sector still dominates the economy and way of life. It is only a billion people of the

First World in the North-Western hemisphere, whose service sector is already their principal economic activity, who are now experiencing the birth pains of postmodernity. In between these two extremes is to be found the Second World of the former communist countries in Eastern Europe which are still in their midindustrial age.

Pulled by the tertiary and quaternary sectors of the postindustrial economy, the postmodern societies of the twenty-first century will change much more than their occupational characteristics. As a result of more information, higher education and greater leisure, people in postmodern societies have more time, energy and data to participate in public affairs. On this basic premise rests our position that politics will occupy a greater time and place in the postmodern world.

On the other hand, the wild material growth of mass industrialism is slowing down due to a large extent in resource scarcity and environmental degradation. As quantitative production decreases, distribution issues increase. In times of economic slowdown and turnaround, social frictions and conflicts are bound to spread. This correlation leads us to the second postulate emphasizing the crucial role played by postmodern politics.

The combination of these two hypotheses paints a much more politicized picture for postmodern societies. Well-informed, yet rather insecure people tend to be quite concerned socially and, subsequently, mobilized politically. This consciousness raising aspect of public education results in what may be called the *polity of social conscience*, a phrase which aptly describes sociopolitics.

This new situation of higher and wider social concern among people creates better citizenship and brings political involvement much closer to its classical roots, which were sadly lost in the mass societies of the intervening years. Thus, as a result of increasing natural constraints, as well as improving cultural technics, human enlightenment is presently reaching the higher stages of political development, as reflected in sociopolitics.

In order to elaborate on this thesis, our study treats sociopolitics as the superstructure of *sociophysics*. This latter concept has been recently revamped as a general theory of natural-cultural metaphors which emphasize the strong relationships among psychological, ecological, and sociological factors in defining the human condition.

On the basis of this theoretical framework, *sociopolitics* looks at its universe of discourse from three different perspectives: informatic, ecologic, and technologic. In effect, these particular aspects give it a three-dimensional image which emphasizes the dense information content of postmodern societies, concerns their fragile environmental context, and reflects their high-tech culture.

Accordingly, this book is organized in three main parts, each of which deals with one of the above aspects of sociopolitics. To begin with, the First Part presents the *Infosociety*, as the emerging system of an informatic culture, elaborated in two chapters. Chapter One introduces a model of *Cyberpolitics* resulting from the impact of science and technology on society. Chapter Two focuses on *Infopolitics* as the political impact of informatics on the decision-making process of public policy.

The Second Part concentrates on the *Ecosociety* and contains two chapters dealing with the increasing popular concern for the natural environment. Chapter Three on *Ecopolitics* treats both the internal problems encountered in converting the modern consumer culture into a postmodern conserver society. Chapter Four on *Gaiapolitics* looks on the planet as a whole and the global changes required to attain a planetary ecosystem.

The Third Part elaborates on the *Technosociety* by outlining how political technology can improve democratic institutions. Chapter Five on *Technopolitics* demonstrates how telecommunication and infomediation can revive participatory democracy. Finally, Chapter Six on *Metapilitics* concludes with a conceptual definition of Political Development as the civilizing process of humanity.

These three parts with their six chapters present the principal parameters of sociopolitics as the emerging phenomenon of political development in postmodern societies. As such, the contents of this book could be read either as chapters in the order presented, or individually as self-contained essays, depending on the specific interests of the reader. In any case they should give a good idea of the particular direction that human societies might take in the foreseeable future.

PART ONE

INFOSOCIETY

CHAPTER ONE

Cyberpolitics

System Model of Science, Technology and Society

The impact of science and technology on society is undeniable. The advances of empirical knowledge and its social applications have changed mankind's way of life dramatically. This change has brought about great benefits for people, but at the same time has created grave problems, both for individuals and groups.

Whether looked upon as positive or negative forces, science and technology cannot be ignored as agents of social change. The relationship between these forces and human life has therefore become the critical link in understanding how modern society works. With such understanding, we are better able to inform, adjust and control its complex mechanism and thus create a better postmodern world.

The concepts of information, adjustment and control form the core of cybernetics. More specifically for our purposes, cyberpolitics is the civil process of social communication and control, whose importance is so basic that we have chosen it as the topic of the first chapter of this book. On that basis, we can lay the foundations of sociopolitics within the context of the emerging infosociety in the postmodern world.

In order to do so, we look into the whole picture of the interplay of science, technology, society and humanity. Because of its large scope, our outlook sacrifices detail to generality on the grounds that depth can always be provided after the broad lines have been drawn. For this reason, we have chosen to outline the overall characteristics and dynamics of the emerging postmodern society, and leave their specific applications in particular cases to other studies.

The following presentation sketches the most significant elements concerning the intricate relations and interactions among various social factors. In order to clarify this highly complex content, we are going to utilize the systems theory and method. Therefore, each section of this essay analyses one aspect of the social system, concluding with a synthesis and evaluation of the whole.

System

We begin with a brief outline of the systems method, which should give an overall picture of how we plan to treat our subject matter. As is well known, systems theory looks at reality as a network of interconnected parts. In order to study any of its aspects, one must distinguish those parts which are central to the discourse from those which are of peripheral interest and finally the externalities which cannot be taken into account at all.

The central themes of the study form the system, and the peripheral elements form the environment. This basic dichotomy determines the focus of the research and delineates its parameters. In a first approximation, the system may be defined as a number of interrelated elements. If the system is dynamic, its elements interact and if it is open, it also interacts with its surrounding environment, thus having inputs and outputs.

Accordingly, the minimal requirements for a system consist of at least two elements and one connection. These two requirements form the structure of the system, that is its static attributes. Beyond that, some systems also exhibit a degree of activity, that is behavioral characteristics, thereby manifesting some dynamic action and useful function. In that case, they perform an operation which converts inputs into outputs, thus playing the role of a transformer.

The kind of systems that we are dealing with here show all these characteristics. Seen as a system, society is composed of many disparate elements, surrounded by the natural environment. The structural elements of the social system are the people and their institutions. It is they who determine the functioning of the system within the constraints imposed upon them by nature.

The structural and functional categories of the system are clearly differentiated in the matrix below. This dichotomous differentiation serves as the first criterion to distinguish between social actors and their actions, or between the relatively constant and variable factors of the system.

The other dichotomy of the matrix serves as the criterion of salience which identifies the focus or locus of social activity. The former are the centers of high energy, whereas the latter are the channels that transmit this energy among the various centers. The nodes of social activity coincide with the concentration of institutions and the roles which they play in the system; whereas the ties connecting these nodes set the inter-relations and guide the interactions between them.

Intersecting each other, the above two criteria form the vertical and horizontal dimensions of our matrix, producing four (2x2) mixed types of elements: actors, actions, relations, and interactions. The bulk of this chapter is devoted to elucidating these four concepts, so the following four sections treat each one in turn.

System Matrix

SALIENTS / ELEMENTS	FOCUS CENTERS	LOCUS CHANNELS
STRUCTURES STATICS	ACTORS (UNITS)	RELATIONS (CONNECTIONS)
FUNCTIONS DYNAMICS	ACTIONS (ROLES)	INTERACTIONS (FLOWS)

PRINCIPAL COMPONENTS

Actions

As an open, dynamic and functional system, society must have certain inputs, outputs and feedbacks. The inputs provide the system with the necessary materials and energy to maintain its structure and carry out its functions. The outputs are the surplus products, by-products and refuge which society exports to other systems or rejects into the environment. Finally, the feedback is the information or reaction which comes back into the system as a result of its own actions.

In order to perform these three indispensable functions, the social system has developed the structures which will be mentioned in the next chapter. To begin with, there are the economic functions which extract from nature or import from other systems, material and energy resources to fulfill the needs of society. Insofar as it is able to do so, the economy transforms raw materials into goods and energy into services, which it then exchanges and distributes to the system.

Most of the products of the economy are consumed by the cultural sector of society. That is to say, they serve to feed, house, clothe and move people. By fulfilling these basic human needs, the economy provides the culture with the infrastructure upon which human desires can be manifested and implemented. By consuming the products of the economy, the system's cultural sector can help people communicate, create, play and develop their potential.

In addition to the production and consumption function of society, a third requisite of the system is regulation. Feedback systems are self-regulating because they can adjust their behavior to optimize their functions. To do so, they must have a cybernetic mechanism which can govern their inputs and outputs. This mechanism is, in effect, the social polity.

Governing a complex social system is not an easy matter, so it is done with various degrees of efficiency and efficacy. Collective decision-making and conflict-resolution take a lot of time and energy, thus the political process absorbs an increasing amount of social resources. The development of science and technology has contributed to the problems of government by making society a much more sophisticated, yet delicate system.

The scientific revolution and its dramatic applications in everyday life even within the present generation changed the face of society and affected all aspects of human behavior. More specifically, science and technology transformed both the economic and cultural sub-systems by increasing the quality and quantity of production and consumption in society. As a result, these social changes have created both problems and opportunities for the polity trying to maintain control over the changes according to some rational policy.

Actors

The component units of the social system are its people. The people, members of society, act either individually or collectively to promote their interests. In complex, large social systems, collective action is more effective than individual, so interest groups become powerful institutions of ubiquitous presence.

Social groups are formed and maintained whenever there is enough common interest shared among a distinct number of people. Such groups may be found for every special and particular interest in society, be it economic or cultural. The former are those groups which primarily share production or exchange interests, such as industrial, agricultural, financial and commercial institutions. The latter are those sharing consumption or expression interests, such as families, clubs, schools, studios and churches.

Since this study is particularly interested in science and technology, we must distinguish those groups concerned with these aspects of social life. Although such groups could sometimes fall under either the economic or cultural category, we should here make a clear differentiation between them.

In the scientific sector are those groups which create or discover information or knowledge. The main examples of this type are research institutes or test laboratories as well as societies for the advancement of science. In the technological sector are the groups which develop and adapt the scientific discoveries to practical applications. The institutions in this sector are engineering companies and innovation firms as well as associations of inventors and technical experts.

So far, we identified two dyads of collective actors making up the postmodern social system. On the one hand, there are the economic and cultural groups and, on the other, the scientific and technological ones. These four kinds of actors, however, are supplemented by a fifth, in a class by itself.

This actor is the state, or the authoritative sector of society. The institutions of this sector are the official agencies of the government, as well as the legislative, executive and judiciary bodies of the social system. It is only by specifically including them that we complete the list of the five protagonists of modern society. As far as we are concerned, these five groups are the necessary and sufficient components of the info-society we are trying to describe. To illustrate what has been said so far about the structures and functions of the five principal elements of our social system, we present the drawing in the next page. The five legs of the star represent the Scientific, Political, Economic, Cultural and Technological components of society. We have thus named this stylized representation the S-P-E-C-T Model.

SPECT Star Model

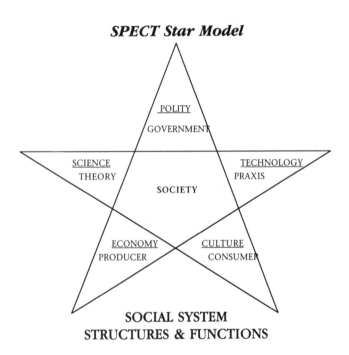

POLITY
GOVERNMENT

SCIENCE
THEORY

TECHNOLOGY
PRAXIS

SOCIETY

ECONOMY
PRODUCER

CULTURE
CONSUMER

**SOCIAL SYSTEM
STRUCTURES & FUNCTIONS**

Relations

According to the SPECT Model, society is composed of five sectors, structurally as well as functionally interrelated. Having described the nature and function of each of these sub-systems, let us now investigate the relationships which tie them together in an all-inclusive social system.

First, it should be recalled that open systems have two kinds of spatial relationships: domestic or intramural and foreign or extramural. The internal relations connect the parts of the system to each other, whereas the external relations tie the system to its environment. Here, we take a look at both kinds.

It is well known that as units increase arithmetically, their interrelations increase geometrically, therefore the more members a system has, the more numerous the relations among them. Beyond a certain number of units, their combinations or permutations become astronomical, according to the factorial formula.

Fortunately, we have aggregated the members of our system into five groups, so that we need only worry about a relatively small number of relations. Moreover, we shall consider only bilateral relationships which run in both directions. With this simplification, we are left with twenty relationships (5 sectors x 2 directions x 2 couples). These internal dyads combine to form our total social network by interconnecting all five sub-systems.

In order to illustrate this network, a revised SPECT Model has been redrawn below. By looking at it, one can easily see the system's twenty interrelations, since each line is a two-way channel. For example, the political sector relates to the economic (PE) x vice versa (EP), to the cultural (PC x CP), to science (PS x SP) and technology (PT x TP), totaling eight relationships. Every other sector is similarly interconnected in eight ways, but since these connections are duplicated the total is only twenty.

In addition to the internal relations, we must also consider the external ones. In this area, we shall take into account only a two-way channel between each sub-system and the environment. For instance, the political sector has an input (NP) and an output (PN) with nature. So does each of the other four, for a total of ten relationships, as shown below.

This network of thirty relationships, along with the nodal points where they cross-cut each other, describes all the significant characteristics of the social system. Of course, not all relations are equally important for our purposes: some are indispensable, while others are irrelevant. This distinction becomes clear later, when we look into the substance of these relationships.

Pentagonal System Network

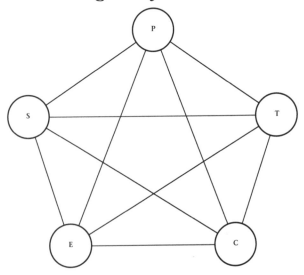

TWO-WAY STRUCTURAL CHANNELS
OF
SOCIAL RELATIONS

Interactions

On the basis of the structural relations worked out so far, we can now superimpose the interactive flows which animate the system. These flows provide the content that fills the channels connecting the five centers of activity in society.

Theoretically, there are three types of active ingredients running along the arrows of the social network model: *material transportation* (inanimate and animate, including people); *energy transmission* (natural and human, including labour); *information communication* (facts and values, including money).

These three interacting aspects of reality are convertible to each other, so that exchanges are possible between them. Since the social system may be regarded as a transformer, it continuously converts one form of reality into another. As we saw, each of the five social sectors specializes in a particular kind of conversion which changes its inputs into outputs, combining matter, energy and information. These combinations produce scientific knowledge, government policy, economic goods, cultural values, and technical tools. The natural environment, of course, provides the resources for all these social goods and receives its discarded bads.

It should be noted that the distinctions made here are relative rather than exclusive. Social functions cannot be precisely separated along institutional lines. So that when we say that the principal function of science is research to increase knowledge, we do not mean that it is its sole function. Social activities are multifunctional as well as multicausal thus their inputs, conversions and outputs include several intended products, accompanying syndromes and unintended by-products.

Nevertheless, for purposes of analysis, we can distinguish a formal activity for each institution and relation. In order to illustrate all these interactions along the connecting channels, the input-output matrix below shows the twenty internal and ten external flows to and from each sub-system. Note that nature is treated here as the sixth sub-system.

The labels in each box are only examples of a central interaction and not necessarily the dominant one. So that an important flow along CE is consumer demand upon economy and conversely, the flow

Social Interactions Matrix

OUTPUTS FROM / INPUTS TO	S	P	E	C	T	N
S	RESEARCH	GRANTS	CAPITAL	PARADIGM	APPARATI	DATA
P	REASON	GOVERN	TAXES	LOYALTY	ARMS	FACTS
E	SERVICE	CONTROL	PRODUCE	DEMAND	INVENTION	RESOURCES
C	EDUCATION	SECURITY	SUPPLY	CONSUME	TRAINING	PEOPLE
T	DISCOVERY	RULE	FUND	NEED	DEVELOP	TEST
N	CONCEPT	MANAGE	WASTE	POLLUTE	GROOM	CONTEXT

INPUT-OUTPUT TABLE

along EC is the supply of economic products to the consumer. The upper left to lower right diagonal of six boxes represents the activities within each sub-system (SS, PP, EE, CC, TT, NN) and therefore are not properly speaking interactions, which only total thirty ((6 x 6) - 6). All in all, the table should give a synoptic picture of the kind of flows running along the arrows shown in the social network.

Process

So far, we completed the presentation of the structural-functional aspects of the SPECT Model. By doing so, we described the activity centers as well as the flow channels of the social system. It now remains to indication of this system operates under certain conditions. To do so, we introduce the time element, which was so far held constant. This means that we shall now follow the chronological sequence of the flow of events among the various sectors in society.

In order to illustrate this sequence of events, we have prepared the flow chart below. The vertical dimension shows the SPECT sectors, while the horizontal shows eight phases in chronological order. These indicate the steps which a typical activity might follow in one cycle of its process.

Since our interest here is the interaction between science-technology, on the one hand, and economy-culture, on the other, with the polity in the middle; the process we want to follow oscillates between each of these sectors in a particular sequence. The particularity, of course, depends on the specifics ofeach case in question.

Nevertheless, what we have chosen to illustrate is general enough to serve as a prototype. In such case, science begins the cycle by some discovery of a 'secret' of nature. This new knowledge is diffused throughout society and, thereby, affects the mental or spiritual culture by destroying old beliefs and creating new expectations.

The political arena here comes into play by debating the pros and cons of the discovery and trying to anticipate its social impact. As a result, it can promote or discourage its further development by regulating its application from theory into practice. If there is enough support, technology takes over to develop some functional implement, useful to the system.

The economic sector takes over next, by mass producing the new commodity for popular consumption. If the market succeeds in selling the novelty to the people, another step in the process of cultural change has been effected. Whether such change is a gradual evolution or a quantum jump, there comes another public debate evaluating the social impacts of the new technology.

As a result, the governing institutions of society will most likely formulate a public policy controlling the usage of the new product or directing new research into its improvement, thus starting another cycle of this ongoing process. Of course, all cases do not follow this scenario in exactly the same steps. Often certain phases may be skipped altogether and others prolonged. Moreover, the process may be short-circuited and return to its origin before it completes the entire cycle. It all depends on the particular factors shaping the progress of each case.

In spite of that, we still think that the model presented here is generally valid. Therefore, it could be useful in noting how particular cases compare to it, either as predictions or postdictions.

Operative Process

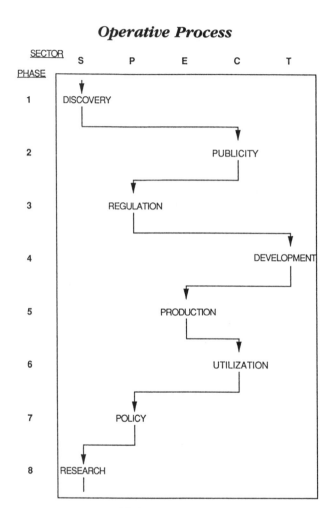

FLOW CHART

Based on a systematic analysis of the structures and functions, relations and interactions, as well as the contents and processes of the social system, we have now concluded this general sketch of the most important parameters of postmodern society. More specifically, we focused on the cybernetic connections of science and technology to economic, political and cultural affairs. Looking at the interdependence of these five areas, we could discern the potential impact that one can have on the others. Finally, we followed the system's cyclical process involving a typical sequence of events.

Since this chapter has been described in a very succinct manner, no further summary is necessary. Nevertheless, we should emphasize the open-ended research potential of this cybernetic model. It is evident that every relation and activity described here can be the subject of a separate study. As the bibliography at the end of the book indicates, many such studies have already been done and others are on the way.

Yet, seen in isolation, specialized research loses the forest for the trees, so it was to correct this problem that the present synoptic study was undertaken. Perhaps, it went too far in the generalized direction, but this was to compensate for the opposite tendency which tends to dominate contemporary research.

As a result of this overview, we should be better able to understand where the various pieces of cyberpolitics fit in the total picture of infosociety. At the same time, we should be able to see the areas where more work has to be done. To this end, the following chapters will contribute to the discussion of the most significant aspects of sociopolitics.

CHAPTER TWO

Infopolitics

Political Power in Infosocieties

As the SPECT model in the previous chapter implied, one of the most dramatic phenomena of the postmodern world is the impact of technology upon society. The practical applications of science have made such great advances in recent years that they have brought about a revolution of unprecedentent proportions. The significance of this revolution is measured by the perceived impact it has on both nature and culture. Technological innovation is bringing about profound changes in our lives by solving many of our problems. Yet, at the same time as it is creating others, thereby presenting us with new dangers, challenges and opportunities.

The social changes brought about by science and technology are nowhere more extraordinary than in the way we formulate and communicate information. Within a generation, television and computer alone have revolutionized our culture to the extent that they are now creating what has been called informatic or Infosociety. It seems that in this new society, no area of human life will remain unaffected. Because the effects of information technology are both extensive and intensive, they concern society as a whole and must be dealt with by public as well as private institutions.

In this respect, the interest that information technology raises on politics is rather obvious. Anything which affects society so much cannot but have great political repercussions and involve the government of the country. It is for this reason that we have here undertaken this study of the most crucial interfaces between the politics and informatics of postmodern societies. This chapter investigates various relevant relationships of these infopolitics from the point of view of four different dimensions:

Topical: systems analysis of structures and functions;

Temporal: social dynamics of recent trends and future scenarios;

Spatial: geopolitical perspectives of various territorial levels;

Procedural: prescriptive outline of the policy-making process.

Of course, these dimensions intersect and interact with each other, but they are treated separately in the following sections.

Politics and Informatics

Human reality may be understood as a complex net of systems. This network is composed of interconnected and interacting structures and functions. In order to study this complexity, we can discern three interrelated worlds of reality:

Personal: the intrapersonal world of the human spirit or psyche;

Social: the interpersonal world of human relations;

Natural: the extrapersonal physical and biological environment.

In this study we shall concentrate on the middle or social world and touch upon the other two only peripherally. Even so, the number and complexity of social relations and activities necessitate a further breakdown of society into:

Cultural: the way of life and collective behavior of people;

Political: the process of conflict-resolution and decision-making;

Economic: the production and exchange of goods and services.

Here again, our focus will be on the middle or political system, because of the central role it plays in society. The political, like any open and dynamic system, exists and operates by receiving, converting and transmitting various inputs and outputs from and to its environment. These systemic flows may be distinguished as:

Matter: raw material resources of physical nature;

Energy: high potentials of activity-producing agents;

Information: symbolic signals on the ambient conditions.

A final concentration of the scope of our inquiry will be on the information process and how it is related to the political system.

In the first part of the study, we consider the connections between politics and informatics. The basic hypothesis here is that there are significant relationships between political and informational systems. Moreover, we postulate, these relations become crucial in social systems of high information flow and content, that is infosocieties. The following two sections explain first the political and then the informatic system. On that basis, we then combine the two in a politics-informatics complex which serve as the central model of the study. Finally, we look for the major implications of these structural relationships and the issues they bring forth.

The Political System

We define politics as a human activity aimed at civil
conflict-resolution and public policy-making. In this
context, civil means a social interaction regarding
public affairs in which there occurs a dialectical
exchange of influence or power. Since power is the
ability to do work, political power is the capacity to
get people to do something. This capacity characterizes those who can influence others to behave in a
certain way. The powerful can do that by convincing
people that what they propose is necessary or desirable for the common interest.

On the basis of these definitions, the political system is that sector of society in which collective decisions are made as a result of the interplay of various
forces. The political system converts differing views
and opposing interests into a policy consensus by a
process of equilibration and compromise. An important problem in politics is to locate the foci in which
these activities take place and the loci along which
influence flows.

For our purposes here, the structures and functions
of the political system are simplified by discerning
two main centers of activity and one channel of influence between them:

State: the authoritative institution of policy-
making and implementing;

Polity: the public arena of issue-confrontation and
accommodation;

Media: the channels of influence flow between
State and Polity.

These two components of the political system and
their interconnecting channels operate by transforming resources and pressures from the social system

and the natural environment into controls and services for people and things. This conversion of inputs into outputs and their subsequent feedback forms a cybernetic cycle which governs large areas of society.

Although this activity affects all people, few engage in it. The polity, supposedly consisting of all citizens, is actually dominated by powerful interest groups and political parties represented by lobbyists and politicians. The State, in turn, is run by a bureaucracy of experts and functionaries who respond to the exigencies of political pressures exerted by its power brokers. The results of this process, therefore, reflects the net remainder of this calculus.

The Informatic System

Information is made up of certain symbols which have some meaning for human beings. Information is used to decrease the areas of our ignorance about reality and hence is indispensable for the survival and operation of social systems. Information makes the world an organized complexity and helps us to understand and deal with it. As such, it builds synergy and counters entropy.

The flow of information in, through and out of a system is an important process, on a par with that of matter or energy. For that reason, a principal characteristic of society is how it collects, treats, stores, recalls and uses information. Society not only produces, exchanges and consumes materials and potentials, but also data. In the last case, the formulation structures and mediation processes make up the informatic system.

A simplified composition of that system would, therefore, include the two components and their interconnective link:

Formulation: collection, manipulation and storage of data;

Communication: selection, translation, diffusion of messages;

Canalization: data transmission flows through the system.

The formulation component is stimulated by the reception of signals from the social and natural environment. It interprets and organizes these signals into meaningful and useful data, some of which it then transmits to the communication component for preparation and promulgation in society.

The structural elements of the informatic system include social institutions, such as research institutes and laboratories, computer companies and libraries for the formulation of information, as well as the mass media, post offices and telephones for the communication of information. The former are staffed by scientists, intellectuals, programmers, calculators and organizers of data, whereas the latter include journalists, publishers, editors, operators and messengers. The significance of these people in society is evident, since they operate the machinery of production and distribution of knowledge throughout the system. Society depends on these information manipulators to manage and operate its vital nervous system as shown below.

The Infopolitics Model

Now that we elucidated the systems of politics and informatics separately, we combine them to form a single complex as illustrated in the diagram. From this figure we can see that the political system is represented by the vertical rectangle while the informa-

Informatics-Politics
Interface Complex

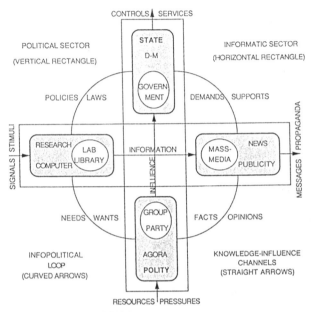

NATURE-CULTURE
(INPUT-OUTPUTS)

tional system is the horizontal rectangle. To emphasize their interrelationships, we have placed them in an overlapping and cross-cutting manner which produces a cruciform, whose four arms correspond to the main components of each system: that is, state-polity and formulation-communication.

This structural system-complex exists and operates within the social and natural environment from which it receives its inputs and to which it transmits its outputs. To begin with, signals from society and nature are collected and enter the informatic system where they are processed and then diffused in three directions: the society at large; the polity and the state. It is the latter two which are of particular interest to us here, since we are dealing with the political impact of information. In this case, information reaches the political arena in the form of facts and opinions read, seen or heard by the politically active public.

On the basis of their education and socialization, people perceive their needs and articulate their wants. These form the public opinion which is picked up by the informatic system reprocessed and transmitted to the organs of the state as popular demands or supports. On this information, the state makes decisions and formulates policies which respond to the popular pressures as presented by the information system. Finally, that system collects, mediates and communicates government policies to the public at large. This information re-enters society and its polity where it eventually becomes the feedback which starts a whole new cycle again.

According to this simplified model of a long and complicated process, the informatic system intervenes at many points between the public and its government. Of course, there are more direct relations between the political arena and the state which bypass the informatic system by using traditional interpersonal contacts. Such communication is decidedly a minor part (less than a quarter) of the total information flow in modern societies. Under these circumstances, informatics play a key role in politics.

Scientia potestas est

At the beginning of this chapter, we made a hypothesis relating politics and informatics. Now, we go a step further and state the main thesis, implicit in the model as tersely put in the Latin dictum above. What we are proposing here is that knowledge leads to power, in the sense that one who has information has a potential to influence people and hence affect their behavior.

Political power proceeds in a dialectical manner. People influence each other by exchanging information, so politics involves the communication of facts and opinions among individuals and groups. It is through such communication that various interests and views become known. Information, thus, influences our thoughts and actions. Without it, decision-making and implementing would be impossible both on a personal and social scale.

It follows that the way in which information is acquired, processed, distributed and utilized in society is of major political importance. As is the case for most things, information is not equally spread among people. Some people are better in formulating and communicating information, so they have an advantage in influencing others. This capacity puts the professionals of information in key positions as the gatekeepers of the flow of knowledge in society. Their activities in collecting, manipulating and disseminating information determines public policy making because they control vital junctions along the political process.

Of course, the political system is influenced by many factors in addition to information. The cultural system with its values and customs, as well as the economic system with its ownership of the means of production and distribution, have a lot to do with political power. But, according to our thesis, the Informatic Society places a particular emphasis on knowledge and hence tends to concentrate extraordinary power on those who control the instruments of education and the channels of communication. Those who have useful information, therefore, rank along, if not above, those who possess scarce resources in dominating the way society shares its costs and benefits.

Infopolitical Power

From what has been said so far, it seems that the relations between politics and informatics are both structural and functional. The infopolitical interface is structurally established by the connections between the institutions and people in these two systems. Animating these structures and persons are the interactive processes according to which they function. This analysis leads to certain basic questions whose answers should explain what exactly is the politics-informatics complex and how it works.

As to structure, the central question is who has power in this complex. The distribution of power is a primordial question of politics and identifying the power holders is the first task of the political analyst. In our model, we have identified four estates of power: the politicians as power-brokers; the bureaucrats as administrators; the scientists as thinkers; and the communicators as popularizers. It is in these groups where one finds the main actors and principal roles in the arena of politics and informatics. The question is who influences whom under what circumstances? These power relations extend beyond this complex to the social environment and particularly the economic system, where there is to be found another important center of power.

After this identification of actors and arenas comes the investigation of power and control. We have already mentioned some ways, such as control of the access to information, shaping the content of communications, participating in the decision-making process, selecting public issues, etc. Since he who has information has potential power, those who control the media and the messages can influence the inputs to public policies. Such issues as freedom of information, government censorship, ideological propaganda, commercial advertising, secrecy of communication, and intelligence gathering are all crucial in society.

Obviously, how information is formulated and communicated makes a big difference on how influence flows through the system. By manipulating the quality and regulating the quantity of information, one can in effect control policy-making. If such control is concentrated in the hands of a few people, the distribution of both power and information will be uneven. Furthermore, the lines of this inequality could coincide with those of material wealth and poverty, thus exacerbating social imbalance and resulting in political instability.

Technological Trends and Impacts

So far, we have established the structural and functional relationships between informatics and politics in a so-called Infosociety. The suggested model of these relationships supported the thesis that knowledge is power and concluded by defining the evidence that would confirm it.

Now, we reach behind the informational system to consider the technological system underlying it. Technology provides the infrastructure for information in the Informatic Society. What has already been said assumed implicitly such technological basis. Presently, we go on to make the explicit connection between technics and politics.

To do so, we infuse technics into our model. Technology exists in society and more particularly centers around the cultural system; nevertheless, it has direct links with the economic system and indirectly with the political. Our first hypothesis, then, discerns the existence of some relationship between technics and politics. It is on this hypothesis that we focus our attention now.

Another relationship assumed here is that between technics and informatics. For this we postulate that technology affects all three systemic throughputs: matter, energy, as well as form. As the practical application of science, technology determines how we process matter, energy and information in society. As a consequence, it characterizes, if it does not dominate, the culture of a social system.

Finally, in this section, we introduce the time element in the systemic model. This means that we look at the historical evolution of infotechnology and trace its changing impact upon the political system. From that we can make some alternative projections in the foreseeable future. By discerning certain historical trends and constructing some future scenarios, we may be able to establish diachronic correlations among various factors of informatics, technics and politics.

Technic Revolution and Informatic Society

If we define technics as the systematic employment of rational methods and empirical knowledge to achieve human goals, then we can speak of a technological revolution going on in the contemporary world. Technology has revolutionized the world because of three significant characteristics:

Speed of the pace of innovation and acceleration of change;

Depth of penetration and radical degree of impact on things;

Extent of effect and pervasiveness of scope in space.

On the basis of these revolutionary traits, technology has changed the face of the earth and its continued development is ushering in a new era in world history.

Looking at this evolution in a macrohistorical perspective, one may distinguish three great eras of human society:

Agricultural: minimal use of tools and techniques;

Industrial: heavy use of mechanical instruments and operations;

Technological: sophisticated use of artificial intelligence.

The last generation of the twentieth century has witnessed the transition of modern societies from the industrial to the technical mode. Although the world has various social systems at different stages of this process and even if it is by no means certain that all of them will follow the same steps, there are some advanced societies presently entering the technological age.

For these societies, technology has brought synthetic materials and even life, high concentrations of energy from fossil and nuclear sources, as well as an explosion of knowledge. In that last area, infotechnology is revolutionizing society by:

Automation: replacement of human rationality by robots;

Computerization: manipulation of large quantities of data;

Telecommunication: transmission of signals over long distances.

The combination of these functions in informatics and telematics could transform the world into a vast network of high infotechnology. Informatic Societies will occupy the nodes of this network and as such they will spend most of their time and efforts in collecting, processing and dispensing knowledge. As the energy and material needs of people are satisfied by agricultural and industrial technology with a minimum of human effort; information becomes the major preoccupation for most people, most of the time and thus dominates the cultural, economic and political aspects of advanced societies.

Information Technology and Political Change

From what has been said so far about the relationship between technology and society, it would be justified to formulate another thesis for discussion: that is, technological innovations lead to social change and by extension to alterations in the power configuration of social systems. More precisely, the development of infotechnology is changing the political system in some relevant ways. According to this thesis, we consider technics as the independent variable and politics as the dependent. Significant variations in the first factor eventually affect the second.

Of course, technology is neither the first nor the only factor of social change. It operates in conjunction with many other intervening variables in the complex-dynamic system that is society. As such, it affects and is affected by other factors including politics. Here, however, for purposes of analysis, we shall isolate the part of a chain of causation which runs from science and technology, through culture and economy, to government and politics.

Because it opens up new problems and opportunities for action, technology alters economic relations and social structures, and brings political forces into play either to restore the status quo or to find a new equilibrium. By revolutionizing the formulation and communication of knowledge, infotechnology has altered the strata of society in the following ways:

— Creating new information-elites in the techno-cratic complex;
— Broadening the middle-class and raising expectations by education;
— Strengthening mass manipulation by ideological propaganda.

The common thread in all these changes is the increasing capacity of technology to spread information throughout society. The problems which accompany this formidable capacity arise from the unequal quantity and uneven quality of information distribution to various social groups and classes.

This inequality of distribution leads to unequal participation in public affairs and inevitable unequal influence in the political decision-making process. Since technological change benefits some social groups more than others, it is bound to be supported by certain people and opposed by others. The resulting clash of interests and opinions dominates the politics of societies undergoing the infotechnological revolution.

The Technocratic Scenario

Assuming the continued increase of technics and informatics, coupled with an unequal distribution of their benefits, we arrive at a technocratic type of the Informatic Society. This kind of society would be characterized by high technology controlled by a knowledge elite which dominates the body politic and informatic system. The resulting scenario is that of a centralized technocracy deciding the content of information and regulating its flow in society.

Many trends so far are pointing in this direction and further tendencies will accentuate them. As technology becomes more sophisticated, society becomes more complex, hence, requires great expertise to run it. Large complicated systems are costly and fragile, so it takes great skill and will to govern them. Since only few people have such talents or ambitions, few acquire the power to operate such delicate machinery as that of the Informatic Society.

The thesis that technology inherently tends to technocracy, tries to make the best of the inevitable and organize the social system in such a way as to optimize opportunity with necessity. To do so, social structures and functions must be rationalized by authoritative planning by those in the best position to understand and manipulate information. Without such technocratic intervention in society, the system will get out of control and everybody will suffer the consequences.

If a combination of technological and political developments lead to this neo-platonic scenario, one can expect many benefits for the common man. Presumably, government by experts will be very efficient in providing the greatest happiness for the greatest number. Based on benevolent utilitarian principles, a Technocratic Society might be a utopia of sorts and at worst the lesser evil compared to other possibilities.

On the other hand, technocratic control of information precludes participation by laymen in the decision-making process of society. Although technocrats may give people everything else, they cannot give them political power because that would negate the whole system. The masses must accept the leadership of their elites, as long as the system makes their life comfortable. While the automated economy provides the bread, information technology will produce the circuses in this best of all possible worlds.

The Democratic Scenario

In contradistinction to the Technocratic Society, the democratic scenario provides an alternative interpretation of recent trends. These, in conjunction with certain factors, may develop into a more democratic society where participation of the people in public policy-making is optimized. In a democracy, the political system takes collective decisions as a result of social consensus of informed and involved citizens.

Infotechnology can help democracy by spreading information far and wide. The Informatic Society can also be democratic if its population is highly educated and responsible. Educated people are more demanding and hence more difficult to govern. Better informed people want to use this information in making decisions, so they wish to participate in the policies which affect them. As technology solves economic problems, it allows people more time and energy for other things. If this new leisure is not all used in escapist entertainment, some of it is bound to spill over into politics. When it does, society will become much more politicized and public affairs could become the main occupation of the citizen.

This thesis that informatization leads to politicization, assumes that information is the great equalizer when properly distributed. This means that the communication channels will be two-way and multilateral, so that more people can talk to each other. Information technology can facilitate such exchanges by decentralizing its apparatus and becoming accessible to all citizens. Unlike industrial technology, information technology need not be heavy-handed or concentrated; egalitarian polytechnics is a real alternative to authoritarian megatechnics.

Of course, people cannot become experts in everything in order to participate in the political system. Technical questions will have to be decided by specialists, but there is still room for decisions by generalists on the broad issues of public affairs. Societal objectives and cultural values can be democratically determined by the appropriate infotechnology. Through such technology, it would be possible for the first time in history for all the people to become sufficiently informed as to attempt responsible choices. Thus, if we could develop the proper political technology, we should solve one of the most elusive problems of humanity.

Technics and Politics

The general conclusion so far is that technics increase the importance of politics because technological innovation brings about social change; which, if it is not to get out of control, requires collective decision-making. Such process, in turn, requires high quality information, which only technology can provide. Thus, it is easy to see how infotechnology affects political activities.

On the basis of these preliminary conclusions, further work is needed to discover more detailed correlations between technics and politics. Obviously, the relationship is a complex one and involves many intervening variables of economic and cultural nature. An important question here would be what happens to the distribution of power as a society moves into the technological era. Is it possible for the political status quo to survive a technological revolution?

To answer these questions we must study the historical record and establish the trend of events. The history of science and technology can provide examples of dramatic social changes involving politics. Historical trends, of course, can be interpreted in many ways depending on the paradigm or ideology used. Nevertheless, the attempt must be made in order to articulate diachronic correlations. It is on these apparent trends that we base social forecasting. Trends may continue or change as a result of various factors. For that reason we must construct different scenarios to cover the main probabilities. The two we have presented here are only outlines of one alternative between technocracy and democracy. Other combinations may be worked out in greater detail using different factors as variables.

Optimism or pessimism is a function of anticipations and aspirations. In the field of infotechnology, either outlook would depend on whether a way can be found to handle economic scarcity, social inequality and political equity. This last issue involves political technology, which through such innovations as televote referenda, community teleconferencing, and interactive telecommunications may succeed in turning the tide from technocracy to democracy.

Geopolitics and Infoeconomics

Having set the theoretical framework within which the correlations among informatics, technics and politics, may be studied, both in structural and functional terms; we can now apply it in the case of contemporary states, as particular applications of the general principles enunciated above.

To do so, we must introduce another dimension to the model. In addition to the *topical* (structural-functional) and the *temporal* (historic-futuristic) aspects, we presently involve the *topological* field. This means that we look at our topic from the point of view of geography and deal with various issues in different areas. Since our topical focus is politics, the infusion of geographical considerations combines to form geopolitics. The informatic system will henceforth be seen from a geopolitical perspective.

This orientation is organized according to spatial levels of hierarchical relationship. That is to say, we divide the world into several political levels of jurisdiction and study each one separately. In this case, the most acceptable levels are the following:

Intranational: public affairs of local communities.
National: domestic and foreign affairs of one state;

International: relations and interactions in the world.

From this point of view, a country illustrates the national level and thus determines what is internal and what is external activity.

On the basis of these vertical categories, we begin from the lowest level and proceed to the highest. First, we consider the impact of information technology in local communities. Then we move to the national level and its overlapping jurisdictions. Finally, we take a global look at the world as a whole and the problems common to the United Nations system. In this manner, we shall see how our infopolitical model holds up to the realities of the contemporary world.

Infotechnics and Geopolitics

Although rather banal, it is true to say that modern telecommunications have effaced geographical distances. Information technology has made instantaneous communication a possibility for many people spread over large countries. Beyond them, the international telecommunications network is said to have turned the world into a global village.

The political implications of this space shrinkage have made the world more *interdependent* in information as well as in energy and materials. Transnational corporations are now running the global economy along with international organizations shaping the global polity. In this increasingly interdependent world, national independence or state sovereignty is fast becoming an anachronism.

A most important trend accompanying man's conquest of space and time, is the *centralization* of power. Instant communication gives power centers better control over the periphery and thus marginalizes many people living in remote areas. Moreover, the mass media with their standardized programming, break down local particularities and homogenize the world into a single culture.

From the point of view of a country, a communication network can serve to forge nationalism in the same way as a transportation network serves to keep a nation coherent. A strong centrally controlled press, radio and television establishment can promote a national conscience and unite a sparsely populated country by spreading a single cultural message. Recent history has shown how telecommunications have boosted the work of the political, economic, or cultural propagandist.

The relationship between technology and geography, however, is not so simple. What is happening is that we face various contradictory developments. On the one hand, communications have created not one but many national constituencies, from professional associations to cultural movements. These common interest groups operate nationally and pressure the central government on behalf of their members, thus erasing local boundaries. On the other hand, we are witnessing a resurgence of local community activities and stronger demands for regionalism. The most forceful manifestation of this trend, of course, is parochial separatism.

Here, we discern both *centripetal* and *centrifugal* forces at work at the same time in the same space. Evidently, these opposing tendencies create great stresses on the social system of any level. In time, perhaps, one or the other of these trends will prevail, but meanwhile we must contend with both. In any case, subnational autonomism and transnational corporatism may coexist for a long time.

Localization of Informatics and Micropolitics

One of the most serious effects of the information explosion in the mass media is the *anesthetization* of people. Information overload and escapist entertainment promote public apathy and individual alienation. Tuning-in has become synonymous with dropping-out. When everybody can have a personal television set and private computer, one no longer needs anybody. Interpersonal communication deteriorates as man-machine interactions proliferate. Ultimately, society becomes atomized and community breaks down in isolated self-sufficient units.

The political implications of this "mass society" and the "lonely crowd" are significant. As the social fabric disintegrates, politics retreats to small enclaves of power brokers and demagogues. Small elitist groups dominate the political system and dictate their terms to the government. This state of affairs is worse in some countries than in others, but there are many disturbing signs confirming the dictum that a little knowledge is a dangerous thing.

At the same time, there are some signs which point beyond it. As people become more informed and educated, they are more aware and more interested in what is going on. The consciousness raising function of information technology leads to *politicization* of the people. Many are no longer content to be passive onlookers or even periodic voters of a distant government. They demand more immediate and direct influence in matters of everyday life. Traditional representative politics, thus give way to direct and local democracy.

Infotechnology can help this trend as much as hinder it. If the huge mass media empires are supplemented with community-controlled local stations, citizens groups can increase their say in public affairs. When each community is able to process its own information, it will be able to arrive at its own decisions and individuals will feel that they have contributed directly to them. *Participatory politics* could, therefore, become a result of the proper information technology.

This would be particularly helpful in large heterogeneous countries where local cultures resist national assimilation. Such localism, of course, is dangerous because it may break down a country altogether. The challenge is to find a point of equilibrium between community and society that will satisfy both individual fulfillment and collective aspirations.

National Politics and Informatics

The critical political issues in a state usually revolve around two cross-cutting axes: the *national-local* and the *public-private*. The former confronts conflicting jurisdictions between the higher and lower governments; whereas the latter is a power struggle between the political authorities and private or sectoral interests. The geographic cleavages sometimes coincide and other times overlap the functional divisions of various pressure groups, but it is in the interfaces of both where national politics focus.

National-regional conflicts have always been part of any political history, they seem to have accentuated lately. One hypothesis here is that infotechnology had a lot to do with that. Naturally, traditional constitutions could not have foreseen the tremendous innovations of technology, especially in communications, so they left a lot of room for interpretation as to which level of government has what jurisdiction. Contemporary constitutions faced these issues but have hardly resolved them. Regions, of course, demand a more decentralized system, while the nations try to keep and consolidate the gains they made from technological developments.

To compound these problems are those arising from the birth and spread of the new information and communication industries. Both public and private interests are involved in these enterprises in both the provincial and federal levels. Conflicts among different private groups, as well as between private and public interests, reflect the shifting power maps of developed countries. Added to these, are the conflicts between labor unions and management over the issue of automation. Altogether, they make a very complex picture of the contemporary political landscape.

It is evident that the evolving information system has had a heavy impact on the political system of any advanced country. The tendency of technology to multiply power has created large agglomerations of political influence operating in the public and private domain, as well as at the various levels of government. The big three of national politics —*government, business, unions*— have all been strengthened by infotechnology and will continue to be, if certain trends go on. Only the counter trends of community power and popular participation can check such concentrations of power.

Nations in the International System

We have now arrived at the highest geopolitical level where power politics is supposed to operate at its purest. At that level, the interstate system is composed of almost two hundred states; whereas the international system has ten times as many nations. Therein lies one of the main problems of the modern world: that is, the overlaps between the geopolitical and sociocultural divisions create severe stresses and strains in the global system.

At the same time, states and nations are overlaid by hundreds of intergovernmental organizations (IGO), as well as thousands of non-governmental organizations (INGO) and transnational corporations (TNC). Thus the political, economic, and cultural power of the global system is spread over all these actors, unevenly to be sure, since only the powerful few are protagonists, while the others are merely a supporting cast.

Like the national scene, the international system has been greatly affected by infotechnology. Traditional diplomacy has all but disappeared with the advent of instant telecommunication connections among all the capitals of the world. World politics already operates under the computerized surveillance of space satellites. Technology has revolutionized the intelligence field and has erased political borders for purposes of information communications. Under the circumstances, keeping secrets and hiding actions has become almost impossible.

These developments are not limited to macropolitics but have spilled into macroeconomics. Technological capacity is becoming the most important factor of economic wealth, so powerful states rely on it to maintain their advantages. If a state is to maintain or improve its competitive position in the world, it must be at the forefront of technological innovations, particularly in the field of information. Much more than raw materials and energy, information has become a nation's main resource in the postindustrial world.

Now, as never before, smaller countries have to compete much harder in order to survive in a world of giant states and corporations. The international system of superpowers and political alliances, together with the transnational system of corporations and trading blocs leave very little room for small players. Only strategic combinations of public and private resources, central and local governments, can ordinary nation-states keep up in the power competition with multinational corporations and supranational communities.

The centralizing tendency of transnational technology is not only putting advanced countries at a disadvantage. The repercussions on poorer states have been even more severe. The well known gap between the North and the South is nowhere as wide as in infotechnology. Once left behind, underdeveloped countries have no way of catching up without the cooperation of those ahead of them. The demands for a New International Order reflect the frustration of the people of the Third World not only for the economic injustices they suffer but also for the present information maldistribution that leaves most of humanity in ignorance and isolation.

Geography and Technology

The relations between geopolitics and infotechnics are, as we have seen, both sufficiently important and complicated to warrant further investigation. A fundamental question here is how to distribute power and information along the various geopolitical levels: local, regional, global. It seems that technology has made the nation-state too big to solve local problems and too small to solve global ones. Caught in the middle, national governments are attacked by community groups from below, as well as transnational corporations from above.

In postmodern countries, politics is shaped by geography and modified by technology. As infotechnology develops further, many questions arise as to its impact along the national-regional, public-private, labour-management and geographical-functional interfaces, because it is around these cleavages where power-interests clash. Certain technological innovations favour one of these sides rather than the other, thus upsetting the delicate balance of power which only further political maneuvering can reestablish.

In the global scene, power-politics is played through similar cleavages: rich-poor; national-transnational; international-supranational. The problems which have arisen as a result of unequal technological distribution exacerbate geopolitics and require innovative solutions. Will infotechnology tend to concentrate wealth and power in the hands of an international elite who will dominate by manipulating the masses? Will the asymmetric interdependence of the world increase in proportion to the gap between the information-rich and poor people? These are important questions for those who want to study a New International Order.

The different impacts of information technology on space and time pose many dilemmas on the student of politics: centralization vs. decentralization; independence vs. interdependence; nationalism vs. cosmopolitanism; regionalism vs. functionalism; revolution vs. evolution. These apparent alternatives must be considered by the social scientist in order to understand and deal with social change. But, these options may be complementary. As a recent slogan proclaims, "Think globally, act locally — think ahead, act now!" The best policy might be: Local and rapid action on the basis of globalistic and futuristic thinking.

Public Policy in the Infosociety

The fourth and last part of this study, looks into the policy-making process in an ideal Informatic Society. Here we are explicitly choosing a particular future scenario which is considered more desirable than other possible ones; thereby introducing a value judgement and preference for what we already mentioned as the Democratic Scenario. Now we move on to elucidate the political processes which could take place in such technological social system.

So far we have considered informatics and technics as the independent variables which acted upon politics. Such a cause-effect arrow, however, is only part of the story in the contemporary world. As government increases its intervention into the social system, its policies become independent variables shaping the development of technology or the flow of information. In fact, this becomes a loop where technological progress brings about social change which then affects the political system, thereby forcing it to respond with certain policies which in turn determine the further evolution of infotechnology.

Our thesis here is that politics becomes more important as we move into the technological era and construct an Infosociety. The complexity of modern systems and the dynamics of social change require more careful cybernetic mechanisms to keep society in good operating order. Sophisticated systems are quite delicate and fragile, so they must be handled expertly and thoughtfully by the proper institutions. The social structures and functions of control thus become crucial. If control is not to become dictatorial or technocratic, the political system must be strengthened and the policy-making process improved.

This is what we attempt to do in the following sections. In doing so, we construct an ideal procedure for policy-making which focuses on the role of information and technology in this process. For that purpose, we utilize the information-politics complex model introduced at the begining of this chapter. Based on the structural components of that model, we outline a step-by-step sequence which follows the various phases of policy-making and end with a prescription for an optimal interaction among politics, technics and informatics.

Information and Political Technology

The proposed model procedure is based on certain fundamental assumptions which relate politics and informatics. One is that citizen participation is the fuel of political life and the other is that information is the basis of rational action. Our very definition of politics presumes some public involvement in collective decision-making, in the same way as any purposeful activity can only result from processing information as well as matter and energy. Juxtaposing the politic and informatic processes, it is evident that rational politics requires sophisticated informatics. On the contrary, the politics of ignorant masses is an ochlocracy; whereas the activities of esoteric elites is a technocracy.

In an effort to combine informative action and knowledgeable involvement with as wide a popular participation as possible, we outline three phases of the democratic process in an Informatic Society.

Identification: perception and conception of reality;

Intention: volition and decision to do something;

Implementation: execution a controlled activity.

Accordingly, everyone is engaged in at least one of these actions at any particular time, either by forming impressions, trying to arrive at a decision, or expressing oneself. Information comes in at many points along this process, but particularly in the first stages, where technology can have its greatest impact.

In the context of an Informatic Society, both the informatic and the political system alternate in their involvement at all three stages. As is shown in the flow-chart, the two foci of the information system: formulation and communication, correspond to the series of boxes A and B; whereas, the political system's polity and state are represented by boxes C and D respectively. Steps number 1 and 2 belong to the identification stage, 3 and 4 to the intention stage, 5 and 6 to implementation.

As we descend the chart, we meander across the various phase functions of the four arenas undergoing through six cycles of the policy process. By the proper use of both information and political technology, we should be able to optimize policy-making in a democratic Informatic Society. The following three sections, elaborate each phase of this process.

The Infopolicy Process

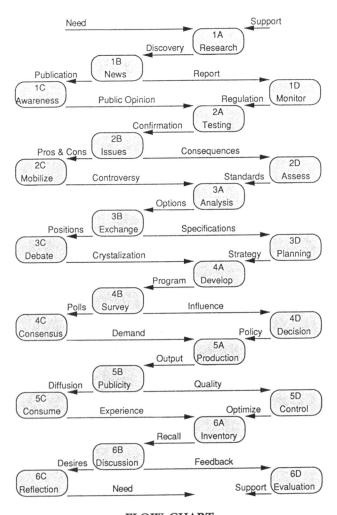

FLOW CHART

Policy Identification

One convenient beginning for the public policy process is at the point when various social needs and political supports meet to trigger an investigation by the research institutions (1A) of the informatic system. These inputs, combined with the intellectual curiosity and knowledge of scientists, could result in certain discoveries which may create as well as resolve social problems. News of the discoveries are diffused by the communications media (1B) throughout society, thus bringing to the attention of those concerned what is going on in the search for knowledge.

As a result of this communication, the political system is alerted to scientific or technological innovations which might be significant to society. A well-informed citizenry (1C) conscious of what is happening around it, forms a tentative public opinion on matters of social significance. Public awareness combined with governmental vigilance (1D), is the first step to good policy making. Government institutions must constantly monitor what is new in the informatic system and together with the initial public reaction determine whether a potential technology should be undertaken.

With a receptive public opinion and incisive state control, tests of new technology could be carried out (2A) and the results confirmed to the media. At this stage, it is the function of the media to determine the issues involved in the innovation (2B) and publicize both the pros and cons to the population. As is the case with most technological innovations, there can be found both advantages and drawbacks according to different points of view. These differences mobilize various (2C) citizen groups either to support or oppose any new technology.

At the same time, government institutions should be making a technology assessment (2D) of the whole project to find out what could be its social consequences. This assessment requires the consideration of norms as well as facts by the political system. Based on the generated data, technology should be assessed on how it would affect the culture of society as a whole in addition to how it might benefit or hurt particular individuals. Programs such as "Ethics and Values in Science and Technology," "Science for Citizens," and "Public Understanding for Science," can go a long way to involve people in such technology assessment.

Policy Intention

The first phase of the policy process is primarily informative: that is, it was designed to sensitize the people to technological issues and thus prepare them to participate in collective decision-making. The second phase enters in the heart of the political process which is conflict resolution. In this phase, the political system converts various opinions and interests into a common policy.

The role of the informatic system here is to make a systematic analysis (3A) of what is involved for a decision to be made. Learned societies and think-tanks study the situation and present the alternatives which are open for selection. These and other options would then be the subject of a public discussion (3B) through the mass media. Public debates in community stations (3C), teleconferencing and other techniques facilitate to widen popular participation in social issues and thus open up politics as wide as possible.

With the help of this public airing of controversial issues, the government machinery can plan its strategy (3D). Alternative plans would thus be made on the basis of both scientific analysis and popular sentiments. Only when these two sources agree should further technological development take place (4A). Once the R & D process is completed, the proper institutions of the informatic system prepare the necessary programs to put the plans into effect. Here again, the public must be consulted for the last time before a final decision is taken.

Surveys of public opinion (4B) should show whether there is a community consensus (4C) for or against a course of action. Consensus-building is the function of a successful political process. Political technology can help this process through delphi, charrette and televote techniques. As people are increasingly called upon to make critical assessments, take sides on public issues, and understand more things, such technology becomes indispensable. The more efficiently this process is carried out, the more effective it will be in influencing governmental decision-making (4D). When this happens, politics will no longer be a spectator sport in which the masses watch complex technical games being played by teams of experts, whom they boo or applaud. Participatory technology could bring everyone into the play and restore meaning to citizenship.

Policy Implementation

Public policy is the result of authoritative decision-making legitimated only by political consensus. Legislation is effective and acceptable to the degree that those who are affected by it have been involved in its decision-making process. It is upon this central thesis of participatory democracy that effective policy implementation is based. Hence, technology has a crucial role in streamlining this political process of the Informatic Society.

If this process is successful, the production of goods and services (5A) will be in line with popular demands and political supplies. In this phase, the informatic system has the responsibility of publicizing the available products (5B) and educating the public in their use. In this way, commercial advertising can be more than mere propaganda urging people to consume one thing or another (5C). Informative publicity by the media along with quality control by the government (5D) make the distribution and consumption of the products of technology a responsible enterprise.

Policy implementation, however, does not end with a successful consumption campaign. If the purpose of public policy is ultimate human development as well as the fulfillment of immediate human needs, society must institute ways of learning from its experiences. This feedback forms the accumulated knowledge or stored inventory (6A) in the collective consciousness of the informatic system of society. It is by calling on this information that the communications media promote public discussion (6B) on the degree of satisfaction or disillusionment with what has been experienced. The informatic system thus helps people reflect on their needs and desires (6C), thereby contributing to the evaluation of the whole process by the political system (6D).

As a result of such evaluation, new needs or wants arise which with the support of public resources begin another cycle of research and development to fulfill. This, then, ends the last phase of the policy process from the point of view of the informatics-politics complex. In this phase, the operation of Science and Technology Courts or Citizen Review Boards complete the implementation process and thus institutionalize anticipatory democracy.

Political Technology

Many problems of complex social systems stem from the fact that political technology has not kept pace with informatic technology. Because of that, as well as other factors, societies seem to be getting out of control, policy responses fail to resolve important issues and governments lose credibility and authority. The technological innovations which are creating an Informatic Society must also be utilized to advance and refine our collective decision-making processes.

It is in this area that much work remains to be done to discover the political innovations necessary to update and synchronize social institutions in the technological era. Since science and technology are at the forefront of social change, we must find ways of harnessing them to serve the common good. This is above all a political process which calculates the weight of opposing interests and opinions to arrive at a consensual compromise. To make this process more efficient, we need the help of appropriate technology.

Such technology will improve the procedures of public information, popular consultation, human interaction, collective intervention, community influence and citizen participation. Developing better public inquiries, opinion surveys, advisory councils, educational panels, legislative hearings, mobilization campaigns, and regulatory bodies; society should be more able to perform technology assessment, problem-management, conflict-resolution, information-processing, communication-exchange and decision-making.

Well-informed and educated people are not content merely to vote for a representative once every few years and let it go at that. They want a more direct and frequent involvement in influencing the direction of social change. Many people now demand a greater say in guiding and planning their future. The traditional politics of *lassez innover,* therefore, are no longer applicable to the Informatic Society.

As the industrial revolution provided the basis for mass society, the technological revolution is making possible participatory democracy. Whether this possibility is realized will depend on our political as well as technological imagination and action. *Homo faber* combined with *zoon politikon* could then usher in the new technopolitical era.

* * *

In concluding this essay we draw the main lines of thought emerging from the four dimensions traversed in this chapter. As a result, we should be able to put them in perspective and orient any further work on the subject.

On the assumption that there is a significant relationship between informatics and politics, it was possible to build a model showing how the structures and functions of the informatic system correlate with those of the political. In effect, information manipulation may be readily translated into political power, so that those who have knowledge can also aquire influence.

This traditional correlation reaches its zenith in the Informatic Society because of the current technological revolution. Technology has enabled some people to formulate and communicate great quantities of information and thus accumulate large amounts of power. If this trend continues, there are many interesting and important possibilities in the near future. Whether one or another of these possibilities materializes depends on how the political system handles technical innovations and informatic structures.

The intervention of public institutions in the shaping of the factors of social change has become evident in all advanced countries. As infotechnology is becoming a major factor of development, it figures more and more prominently both in national and international politics. Governments are forced to consider infotech in their foreign and domestic policies, so as to keep up if not control, the rapid and radical changes it brings about.

For this reason, the capacity of political institutions to understand what is going on and what might happen in this area has to be increased tremendously. If people are to maintain some control of this complex and dynamic world, they must improve their political technology in the same pace as they do their informatic techniques. Such improvement can only come about as people become more conscious and conscientious, thereby devoting greater time and effort to the task.

PART TWO

ECOSOCIETY

Based on the model and agenda set out in the First Part, the Second Part consists of two chapters dealing with the politics of an ecosociety in the turn-of-the-millennium world. Various scientific projections have determined that many current trends lead to an undesirable future characterized by serious ecological, technological, cultural and political crises. Yet these trends need not continue. It is possible to change direction towards a more environmentally stable and sustainable system which is herein labeled *ecosociety*. This analysis aims towards such ideal.

The purpose here is to outline ecosociety's public affairs: manifested internally as *ecopolitics* and externally as *gaiapolitics*. As such, it will specify both necessary and desirable policies an advanced society must adopt in the current world context. The transition from present consumer to future conserver societies will involve certain crucial alterations in both the political processes and the social institutions of these countries as well as of the world at large. Thus, we have to consider the foreign policies of these societies, as well as their domestic politics, most likely to succeed in promoting the desired future.

Our current predicament may be seen as the result of serious failures in three areas:

Ecological, human culture is on a collision course with nature;

Ideological, desires no longer correspond to necessities;

Sociological, institutions cannot respond to increasing pressures.

Because of these critical shortcomings, individual and collective problems are multiplying and solutions become more and more inadequate. In the face of such overwhelming issues, this study will hopefully contribute some realistic positions.

In order to study anything, one should first define the scope and content of its subject. In this case, the scope of ecopolitics covers the main factors of public decision-making in a society where ecological protection in general and resource conservation in particular are paramount. Within this area, politics concentrates on the procedural aspects of public affairs, by focusing on how and why policies are or should be made. It is on the process rather than the substance of policies that we focus here.

To this end, let's begin by observing certain significant historical trends. The world is rapidly entering a critical period manifested by two widening and interlocking gaps: the first, between human culture and physical nature is caused by the effects of technology upon the ecology; the second, within humanity itself exists between more and less developed societies and is caused by their inequalities and inequuities.

Systems break down because they cannot deal with either some external challenge or certain internal disturbance. The present social systems seem to fulfill both conditions by uneven and uncontrolled growth which strains their national constitutions and stresses their international relations.

It is the formidable task of political institutions to control and balance social production, distribution and consumption, so that the whole system does not collapse through violent upheaval or existential nausea. It is suggested that the solution lies in reducing the gaps of malproduction, maldistribution and malconsumption, by recognizing the Earth's finite and fragile nature as well as mankind's essential unity and interdependence.

This thesis may be summarized by three postulates that seem evident at this point:

1. Certain current conditions and trend projections are leading towards a dangerous and undesirable future for the world as a whole;
2. The best non-violent way to reverse undesirable trends is through perceptive awareness, strategic planning, and collective effort;
3. Political institutions are the most suitable centers to provide leadership and mobilize society towards the attainment of common goals.

Any study of the future must be done very cautiously and tentatively. The further away the time focus, the more difficult it is to foresee and forecast; whereas scientific predictions become more accurate as we approach the present. In another sense however, long-range speculation is less constrained than short-range. Wider possibilities open up in the long-run, because more variables come into play, not the least of which are human intentions. Thus, it is much easier to make long-range plans than long-range predictions. It is to the former that politics is most suited.

The future of mankind in the long-run does not exist objectively and deterministically so it cannot be merely discovered by prediction. On the contrary, it is shaped by a combination of unexpected possibilities, objective probabilities, and human volitions.

This last factor multiplied by social power becomes the politics of the future. The shape of things to come is determined by a combination of random, deterministic, and normative factors. Politics deals more with the last mentioned, for this reason the present study is more prescriptive than descriptive, more evaluative than predictive.

The analysis is organized around the internal and external aspects of ecopolitics. The former is the micropolitical level which corresponds to the natural-artificial gap in developed societies; while the latter is the macropolitical level corresponding to the development gap between the Northern and Southern hemisphere. Chapter Three deals with the conditions in postindustrial societies; the alternatives open to such states and their optimal response. Chapter Four concentrates on the international problems of the rich-poor confrontation, the possible international action and finally the option of a planetary ecosystem.

Intersecting this dichotomy, each chapter is divided into three sections following a simplified systems-analysis format. Hence, the first sections deal with the inputs into the system: involving economic, social, and political factors. The second sections point out the various options of policy planning as well as their implementation, which in effect convert the inputs into outputs. Finally, the outcome of this process is outlined in the third sections in terms of the social, ideological, and institutional dimensions of a prototype ecosociety.

CHAPTER THREE

Ecopolitics

Societies in the Postindustrial Era

We begin with a *tour d'horizon* of the current global situation. In doing so, we try to explain how it arose, trace its probable evolution, analyze its sociopolitical significance, and finally propose alternatives for public policy. In effect, we present a diagnosis of our present discontent, a prognosis of where it might lead if strong counteraction is not taken, and end with some therapeutic prescriptions that could improve the situation.

The three sections of this chapter cover successively: the underlying factors of the present consumer societies, the main alternatives open to them in order to change their undesirable ways, and the outlines of the proposed ecosociety. The completion of these three tasks should give a good idea of the political feasibility as well as the rational desirability of transforming a consumer society into a conserver society.

Evolving Conditions

Contributing Factors for an Emerging Ecosociety

This section describes the underlying conditions of the current consumer societies of North America and Western Europe. A proper understanding of these conditions will help in diagnosing the problem and then contribute to its solution. For that reason, it is important to make explicit the assumptions upon which the forthcoming conclusions are based.

To start with, we select techno-economy as the independent variable of contemporary conditions in advanced systems, thus assuming that technical factors determine the phenomenon labeled as the Consumer Society. The following argument attempts to support this thesis.

Economic Infrastructure

The basic supports of the present consumer society may be grouped into three areas: technological innovation, industrial growth, and free market. These areas describe critical processes which have evolved in the last few centuries and will go on unless some equal or greater force deflects them in a new direction. It is upon these initial assumptions that the argument for a new society will be based.

Technological Innovation

Most current social problems are deeply rooted in some peculiar turn that western science has taken in the modern world. The scientific method - which is one way of understanding reality - has brought about certain unforeseen byproducts causing dramatic effects upon social systems. The detachment of the scientific spirit from the objects it studies has neglected the repercussions of its discoveries upon human life. It is only now that enough people became aware of the blatant imbalances which scientific progress has brought about in society.

Defined as the "practical application of science," technology has for the last two centuries changed the face of the earth. The advances of the scientific method and the subsequent benefits of technological production are self-evident and generally accepted as contributions to "human progress." Yet, precisely because of the unprecedented success of technology, the accumulated syndromes now threaten to outweigh any further benefits. What makes the present crisis so insidious is that it is endemic to the technological system, so much so that it is very difficult to separate the disease from its cure.

Many concerned scientists are pointing out that technology harbors a demon who is slowly enslaving mankind because it serves humans only too well. By replacing physical effort with mechanical efficiency, technology makes people feel both pampered and expendable. Hence, we are faced by the paradox of failure-by-success which produces the love-hate relationship of man and machine. The scientific approach, so successful in bending nature to human will, has failed altogether to deal with the dynamic forces of society. The uneven and haphazard development of technology has created so many social discontinuities and economic contradictions that it leads to diminishing returns and could cancel out its many benefits.

Technology has multiplied human power to such an extent that it now commits *hubris* against nature. The modern ethos of unlimited potential decrees that "anything possible is also desirable." By embracing this dictum of technological morality, modern man has allowed means to determine ends. The thoughtless and shortsighted transformation of scientific knowledge into technological know-how has given mankind too much power too soon to be able to use it wisely. For a while it seemed as if this technological euphoria would never end, but it is now evident that man's "Faustian bargain" is due for payment.

Industrial Growth

A direct result of technological applications on a mass-scale has been the phenomenal industrial growth in Western countries. Without belittling the great contributions of industrial technology in improving the standard of living of many people; the time has come to face the increasing social dangers that accompany economic growth. There are, by now, numerous indicators of the destabilizing effects of positive feedback from the industrial complex. This feedback is seriously distorting the social development of the world and threatens mankind with complete loss of control over its own creations.

Industrial development has led to large and complex systems which become increasingly costly and vulnerable to maintain. This tendency of industrial gigantism develops its own momentum in an accelerating rate of supply and demand. The inertia of the techno-industrial complex creates the demand as well as the supply of more and more material goods. This vicious circle alternates between periods of scarcity and plenty, along with rising expectation and nauseating satiation. In general, modern culture creates greater human desires than its industrial capacity can possibly fulfill. Therein lies both the dynamism and danger of artificial growth.

In the organic world, *hypertrophy* is considered pathogenic. Growth is "healthy" only if it follows the typical sigmoid curve pattern, that is, acceleration followed by deceleration. Anything to the contrary is cancerous and usually fatal to the host organism. According to this analogy, uncontrolled economic growth is *carcinogenic* on human culture and should be diagnosed as a major disease of modernity. This accelerating growth places an enormous burden upon social institutions and human constitutions which are inherently slow-moving. The differential rate of change creates a widening gap between the material capabilities of technology and the absorptive capacity of society. We are now reaching the stage when this gap is becoming intolerable.

Organic growth can and will occur as long as the internal capability of the system and the external conditions sustain it. Both these requirements were fulfilled for the last couple of centuries, so that the Western world underwent exponential growth in almost all social sectors. This economic miracle lasted as long as raw materials and fuel energy coupled with technological ingenuity and social organization were abundant enough to fuel it. It would be too much, however, to expect that such a happy juxtaposition of advantageous conditions would last indefinitely.

Exponential growth requires a geometric increase of energy resources and organizational complexity to sustain it. At some point, the limits to growth will be reached when the system inevitably runs out of the wherewithal for further expansion. At that point, growth will have to slow down and reverse. It is, therefore, certain that our way of life cannot continue forever. The only question is when and how this process will be reversed. Its termination will come about sooner or later, either by a series of natural breakdowns or by a social choice of planned transition to a more sustainable system.

The Market System

Turning from production and consumption to distribution, the situation does not look any better. Although technology and industry have undoubtedly brought about mass-production and consumption to some parts of the world, the distributive system has not fared as well. On the contrary, increased production has complicated the problems of a more equitable distribution of the new wealth. The most common solution offered for the problems of maldistribution is further growth. It is hoped that an expanding economy will necessarily improve absolutely, if not relatively, the standard of living of everyone and thus avoid facing the imponderables of distributive justice.

It is true that this expansionist policy has been quite successful as long as the techno-industrial system was provided with enough inputs to keep expanding. The trouble is that the environment cannot provide such inputs indefinitely. The social demands and expectations created by technology far exceed the capacity of the industrial system to respond adequately. Both natural and social forces have now combined to invalidate the thesis of accelerating growth as a permanent solution to social problems.

The simple supply-demand cycle of market economies has been further complicated by the increasing sophistication of the system. In a growing system, complexity increases faster than size. On the other hand, efficiency tends to decrease as complexity increases because of the additional super and infrastructures needed to sustain it. The lowered efficiency then increases waste and exacerbates functional discrepancies.

Finally, the diminishing returns of added growth affect the quality as well as the quantity of goods and services in spite of the increased cost for them. In that case, it takes more effort to induce people to consume commodities than it takes to produce them in the first place, so the costs of distributing and servicing far exceeds the costs of manufacturing.

Moreover, classical economics does not have an overall standard for measuring costs versus benefits to the environment. The application of market criteria to economic policy distorts the allocation of resources in favor of immediate profitable return rather than ultimate social value. In other words, the market is so structured as to continue pursuing private wealth concurrently with the deteriorating quality of public life.

The pursuit for private profit and the competition for relative advantage are carried out at the expense of the common good. Such individualistic behavior creates the paradox of private opulent islands amidst a sea of public squalor. The new type of poverty is not so much material yet, as it is natural and social. It is manifested in acute shortages of health care, public hygiene, overcrowding, pollution, as well as raw material scarcities.

These contradictions of advanced societies, if nothing else, indicate the limits of traditional economic growth. By now, the menacing consequences of uncontrolled and maldistributed affluence has become so obvious as to be questioned even by the most stalwart apologists of the free market system.

The Consumer Society

When we combine scientific technology, mass-industry and the free market, we get the Consumer Society. In order to utilize its technological know-how, this society institutes mass-production methods. In order to justify efficient mass-production, the industrial system must generate sufficient mass-consumption of its products. Once a society gets into this cultural pattern it becomes growth-oriented, novelty-conscious and built-in obsolescent. Its economy seeks continuous over-stimulation by ever increasing demands for more and more commodities which it then meets by further expansion in an ever-widening vicious circle.

This principle of economic growth transforms man into a *homo consumens*, whose main goal in life is to use increasingly large quantities of manufactured products which keep the economy going. Under the circumstances, the economy produces more commodities, so more people buy them and more people produce them. Consumption becomes the end rather than the means of life. People are made into consumption-machines to be fed with colorful baubles and stupefying gadgets which the techno-industrial complex pours out in an ever increasing rate.

There is no doubt that the growth of our producing capacity has gone beyond its original purpose of providing society with the necessary consumption to sustain a healthy life. The self-perpetuating expansion of the economic system is now not only independent of the welfare of the community it is supposed to serve, but has become dysfunctional to human needs. The growth oriented economy has entered a phase of overall dissonance with both the natural and social environment. So much so that an economically "healthy" system, as it is defined now, can only exist by threatening the health of the ecosystem upon which it feeds.

It would be redundant here to repeat the well-known facts of resource depletion and environmental pollution which are the direct, if unintentional, consequences of wild industrial growth. More significant for political purposes is the unhealthy passivity that the consumer society imposes upon people. The affluence of production makes passive consumers out of active citizens. Although, they now have more leisure time in which to do more things, people become spectators of circuses provided by the system. Since production is being taken over by machines, the displaced workers are withdrawing into a rejected state of apathy.

The only positive activity for decision-making which automation has left mankind is the choice among an apparent variety of commodities set out before it by the system. The dubious power consumers are given to select one trademark over another creates in them a false sense of importance and the illusion that they command the complex system which actually controls them. Compulsive consumption, therefore, becomes a consolation to compensate for the inconsequence of their actions and the meaninglessness of their life.

Were it not for the natural laws of the limits to growth, this charade could have continued for a long time, thus burying humanity under a heap of its own effluents. What makes the consumer society's answer to mass production inadequate, however, is that the dosage consumed must be increased progressively in order to keep up with the rising threshold of satisfaction. Otherwise, the consumption addicts would be faced with unacceptable withdrawal symptoms which produce social convulsions. But, as the environment is giving out, social addiction is a prospect that we have to contemplate seriously, unless a program of gradual detoxification is soon put into place. Therein lies the dilemma of modern politics.

Social Impacts

The economic infrastructure, outlined above, gave rise to some serious social syndromes. The new technology which changed the patterns of production, distribution and consumption, indirectly affected the entire social structure of modern societies. This section looks into the resulting cultural crisis and social malaise that now plague the advanced industrial world.

The systemic contradictions and the accompanying widespread dissatisfaction are manifested in many individual and collective ills. Of these, it would suffice to touch upon three areas of current controversy: resource-conservation, wealth-distribution, and citizen-participation. These three public issues have arisen out of the depletion of resources, maldistribution of income and centralization of power. Combined, they have contributed to the dehumanization crisis which now engulfs us.

The Conservation Controversy

The first concrete, specific manifestation of public disaffection with the consumer culture is its growing ecological consciousness This movement has been the result of the mounting concern over the inability of social institutions to channel technological change into the direction of basic human needs.

The belief is now widely held that the continuation of present trends poses grave dangers to the future of mankind. By now, not only scientists but activists and enlightened public opinion has reacted to the energy crisis and the pollution threat so as to make the conservation issue politically correct. Hard evidence in the ecological, physiological and psychological traumas of daily urban life, as well as the popularization of human abuse of nature, have accumulated a critical mass of public concern and pressure which is having visible socio-political impacts.

At the same time, increasingly influential segments of society are questioning the present patterns of production and consumption, demanding that something be done to put some order and responsibility in the market system. The growing consumerist movements and Green parties reflect the public's concern about industrial production and the rejection of conspicuous consumption. This consumer revolt points producers towards meeting people's real needs, rather than pandering to their worst wants. The near saturation of the consumer society with useless commodities shows the growing refusal of many people to work more in order to consume more. The decline of the work ethic and decrease in the quality of life have heightened demands for political action to cure this social disease, rather than merely alleviate its symptoms.

Social change can take many forms, one of which is to stop any further growth of industrial production. Such drastic policy, as is advocated by some naturalists, would perhaps solve the problems of depletion, pollution and consumption in due time. It would, however, create such social dislocations and political opposition as to make it practically impossible. Many self-serving vested interests and our self-indulgent way of life can be expected to kill any move to stop economic growth. The magnitude of political strain resulting from such radical reversal of tradition could not be supported by any liberal democracy.

The conservation controversy, then, is a real dilemma because we cannot go back to a state of nature, even if we admire its simplicity. Since mankind has lost its proverbial innocence, society must use its knowledge. But, at the same time, the environment cannot sustain the increasing production which technology makes possible. It is in the face of this ecosocial contradiction that the present debate is waged.

Distributive Justice

The crisis of resource depletion and environmental pollution brought to the surface an even more politically charged issue: social justice. As long as the economy expands at a good pace, problems of distribution are secondary. Income inequalities are tolerable because overall growth plus social mobility benefit everyone more or less. Even if economic growth is not equally profitable to all the people; those at the bottom can be kept happy by some visible improvement of their standard of living. Based on this principle, rich countries can afford to postpone the thorny issue of wealth maldistribution by constantly increasing the size of the pie to be distributed. Economic growth, therefore, becomes a political necessity in order to maintain social stability.

This precarious stability was maintained by a happy combination of circumstances for a generation after the Second World War. By the early seventies, however, it became evident that this unprecedented prosperity was too good to last. The pressures of diminishing resources, suffocating pollution and social disorder brought about economic complications most dramatically manifested in the modern disease of *stagflation*. This baffling combination of economic stagnation at the same time as galloping inflation indicated that the problem was beyond simple solutions.

As the economy falters and contracts, the issue of who is going to be the greatest loser becomes paramount. Those at the bottom of the scale can no longer be expected to pay the lion's share of the costs without fighting back. Moreover, sharing losses is a much more difficult task than dividing profits. So to an already critical economic situation is added the more touchy political issue of conflict of interests among various powerful groups. An economic depression in a society where labour forces are highly organized and militant is a very dangerous prospect indeed because it leads to general strikes and violent confrontations.

It is for that reason that the economy of highly organized societies must grow at all costs; even if it consumes the very foundations upon which it rests. This dubious solution of artificial stimulation of an economy in order to hide social inequalities evidently pays for present stability by mortgaging the future. The only justification for such policy would be to buy time within which the looming redistribution problems will be tackled and solved. Otherwise, economic growth simply postpones the day of reckoning when a solution will be more difficult to attain. The longer these problems are allowed to fester and accumulate the greater the adjustments to be made and the deeper the human suffering that accompanies the social upheaval which will eventually break upon us.

In an advanced socio-economic system, the problems of production and consumption cannot be treated separately from those of distribution. These three form essential elements of the same balance, each of which affects the others. In this condition of interdependence, the distribution of social and economic resources becomes the ultimate political problem. Distributive justice must therefore be attained not only for ethical reasons of alleviating human suffering here and now, but also for political reasons of maintaining social stability today and tomorrow.

Political Equality

Maldistribution of wealth not only means economic poverty in the midst of plenty but political impotence in the periphery of power. The poor are not only deprived of economic goods but of political influence. They are excluded both from the market and the ballot, so are neither good customers nor responsible citizens. Worse still, political impotence is much more widespread than economic poverty because it spills over into the middle classes.

People who feel powerless in the political arena lose interest in politics and concentrate on their private affairs. The gap between private and public life separating the elites from the masses in society is also responsible for the alienation of large numbers of people from their political institutions. In the face of large and complex organizations, most people feel irrelevant and inconsequential, and as a result become apathetic, if not autistic.

Although the majority may find solace in passive withdrawal from public affairs, an increasing number show their dissatisfaction in active opposition to the system. The rise of criminal activities, civil disobedience, political conflict and general anomy are symptomatic of the breakdown of social order in our times. Many of those who feel excluded from the system and unjustly treated by its institutions have now begun to organize in order to fight back for their rights. This development then translates mere social dissatisfaction into an explosive political situation.

Higher affluence and education combined with a liberal tradition have permitted the organization and proliferation of various interest groups which now are increasing their demands upon society. For that reason, the greatest pressures do not come from the disinherited poor but from the relatively affluent middle class and unionized working class. In particular, it is the intellectuals, the feminists, the professionals, rather than the worst-off, who are most vociferous in their demands.

It is apparent that the politicization of society has lowered the threshold of tolerance in the system. As more people become aware of social inequities and organize to redress them, political confrontations multiply among opposing groups and conflicting interests. The political system must, therefore, try to respond to the new power centers, in addition to the traditional ones. Workers, women, consumers, ethnics, natives, all compete with each other; as well as with the more established regional, professional, commercial, financial and industrial lobbies.

Politically aware and socially involved people are not easy to govern, because they want to get involved in their own government. As more and more people demand to participate in the public decisions affecting them, it becomes so much more difficult to reach the decisions that please everybody. For that reason, political institutions find it increasingly difficult to make controversial policy decisions. As a result of the politics of pluralistic societies, public policies are a compromise at the lowest common denominator of inter-group bargaining. Under the circumstances, social change can only move incrementally and slowly; even if the situation requires more rapid and radical action.

The Dehumanization Crisis

The problems of conservation, distribution and participation are only the most salient points of a much deeper malaise. These social issues reflect more human troubles than political institutions can cope with. Behind them can be found the tools and techniques of modern culture. It is the technological ethos with its scientific management methods, assembly line processes, compartmentalized knowledge and superspecialized education, that mechanize, regimentize, and atomize humanity.

For the sake of more efficient mass-production of standardized commodities, industry fragments and routinizes work into simple mechanical tasks which deaden the spirit of those who perform them. This boring, tiresome and unhealthy work alienates people and transforms them into passive producers and consumers of goods. Such individuals are not only dehumanized but also decivilized and depoliticized. They become *idiotes* in the classical sense of the word.

At the same time, the growth of economic wealth and social affluence has raised the education and expectation of the average person. A higher standard of living does not simply anesthetize people, it also makes them restless, more demanding and harder to please. A well-educated and highly trained labour force is more difficult to control and manipulate. In effect, universal education has led to a short supply of ignorant and servile individuals of the kind needed to man assembly lines. This shortage of morons forces intelligent persons to work far below their potential, thus filling them with resentment, frustration and anger.

The moral and spiritual traumas which result from these conditions are all around us. Many people suffer from a despairing emptiness which sometimes borders on nihilism. They are disoriented in the midst of an incomprehensible world in which they have little faith. People have lost their convictions and ideals, so instead they have turned to mystical religions, apocalyptic visions, and extremist movements.

This is not a pleasant situation and its continuation is fraught with serious socio-political implications. The visible inequities and insecurities of the economic order create egocentric, competitive, yet dependent individuals, who are neither healthy nor happy. The system of distorted production, maldistribution and unsatisfying consumption is directly related to the increasing antisocial behavior of large numbers of people. The human reaction to an oppressive system is amply manifested in absenteeism, sloppiness, sabotage and stoppages in the work-place; irresponsibility, dishonesty and mistrust in the market; corruption, cynicism and loss of confidence in politics; as well as escapism, individualism and isolationism in personal relations, all of which indicate the pervasive disillusionment in the present system.

Public Role

The somber picture just painted is of course a caricature of reality. Focusing on the dark side of modern life shows only one side of the coin, while it omits the other brighter one. Our role here however is not to praise technology, but rather to point out its shortcomings in order to correct them. Constructive criticism serves the purpose of progress as a prerequisite to constructive proposals.

Of course, it is much easier to destroy than to create, so people more readily agree on what the problem is than on how to correct it. For that reason, while the consumer society is widely criticized, there is yet no consensus on what is the alternative. This public controversy creates the proper climate for politics to enter in order to define the needed direction for social change. After setting the agenda of social issues, politics proceeds in an open discussion to generate sufficient support to effect a public policy. This section looks into the crucial role of political leadership, in this path-breaking effort.

Socialization Trend

The complex social systems emerging as a result of techno-industrial development have in turn necessitated greater state intervention and control in all aspects of social life. The twentieth century has been marked by a steady increase of government activism which now permeates even liberal regimes.

This development has been so deep and fast that it generated its proper reaction. Recently, the privatization and deregulation movements have arisen to correct some of the abuses of state ownership. Moreover, taxpayer revolts have deflated government budgets somewhat and citizen resistance has loosened some of its more obnoxious controls.

In spite of these temporary set backs, the heavy historical trends still point in the general direction of increasing social cybernetics. For a multitude of reasons, the polity cannot but become even more significant in the future, as more collective decisions affecting society will have to be taken up in the public arena.

This imposing trend is partly due to the increase of diverse interest groups which make conflicting claims upon society. The state not only acts as a referee among these various pressures, but coordinates their increasing interdependence. Along with the acceleration of social change, there is a rapid rise of social and economic externalities which require assessment and control. The cybernetic function of government, therefore, becomes indispensable to an increasingly complex social system.

It is clear that only the political institutions of society possess sufficient influence to redirect economic growth. Only the polity can mobilize enough popular support to effect sweeping changes in our way of life. The enormous effort needed to develop alternative sources of energy, control pollution, create more efficient industry, change consumption patterns and redistribute the wealth, can only be undertaken by a collective will. No private individuals or groups can independently marshal the costly investment and apply it to future redevelopment. The task must necessarily fall upon the government.

This, however, does not mean that individuals count for nothing in modern society. On the contrary, a citizen's duty under the circumstances becomes even greater. The common attitude of letting the government handle everything, and then blaming it whenever it fails, is both self-abnegating and self-defeating. In the final analysis, people deserve the government they get, so it behooves everyone to accept some responsibility for whatever happens in the polity and act accordingly.

Constitutional Decentralization

Speaking of the *polity* presents some difficulties. Modern Western states usually apportion their functions among central, regional and local levels. This is more so in the case of federations where sovereignty is shared by several distinct jurisdictions and layers of authority. This distribution of power has both advantages and disadvantages. On the one hand, decentralization is necessary for local participation and democratic decision-making. On the other hand, political unity demands that any major social change must have the consensus of all these communities. For a national policy to succeed, it must have the cooperation of regional authorities; the larger ones of which can sabotage the policies they disapprove. For that reason, an effective national policy-making process must ultimately involve regional as well as central governments.

Although most constitutions place state sovereignty in the central government, prevailing political forces emphasize the decentralization of power. Pronounced regional interests and their assertive governments tend to erode effective national control in many critical areas. In order to placate the subnational centrifugal forces that threaten to tear nation-states apart, central governments are often forced to acquiesce to this decentralizing trend.

Naturally, traditional constitutions could not predict the technological developments of the twentieth century, much less their social repercussions, so they did not make adequate legal provisions for handling them. Contemporary states, therefore, flounder in the morass of the unforeseen consequences of changing circumstances.

In the particular goal of the ecosociety, there are many moot points of how the various jurisdictions could cooperate to bring it about. Having one level of government control the land and its resources, while leaving the regulation of water and air to another, makes cooperation between these authorities indispensable for any conservation policy on a national scale. Regardless of the legal niceties, however, an ecosociety will develop according to the ever-changing political configurations within social systems and the environmental constraints outside them.

Administrative Coordination

The growth of modern government is both quantitative and qualitative. The increasing complexity of the social system requires a more complex governmental machinery as well as a larger administrative establishment to implement public policies. The spread of bureaucracy throughout society is a universal phenomenon of our times. It is this aspect of the state, rather than the political superstructure, which has expanded the most and has affected the activities of every citizen. Municipal, regional and national civil services have become growth industries to which no private corporation can compare as to resources and impacts.

The most significant aspect of this development is the accumulation of knowledge and information that public administration possesses and continues to amass. The postindustrial era upon which we are embarking is based on the high technology by which its social systems operate. In this new era, knowledge becomes the most important foundation of power. An incredibly complex system requires highly qualified specialists to run it. It is these experts who know how to make the machinery work and what is more crucial how to change it. Public policies are not only implemented by the civil service, but are also initiated and elaborated by its technocrats. The politicians, in effect, are only given the choice of selecting among a limited number of alternatives presented to them by professionals and ratifying a certain order of priorities suggested by bureaucrats.

Ecology is a particular case in point. Because of the high technical expertise needed to solve problems of resource depletion and environmental pollution, the focus of inter-governmental and inter-departmental bargaining is to be found at the technical level of central, regional and local experts. The urgency and political salience of the ecological issue has shifted the arena of decision-making to inter-ministerial committees of subject-specialists. Once the political level is forced to take up this public issue, working out the solution can only be left to the experts.

In a similar manner, the more difficult aspects of the ecosociety have to undergo the transformation between the technical and the political levels and back again. The administration's role as the coordinator of policy-initiation, as well as implementation, is therefore as important as the government's leading function in the political sphere.

Political Authority

The final significant area of political change to be touched upon, is the widening gap in the relations between the state and the individual. The technological revolution which created bigger and more complex socio-political systems has dwarfed the individual in relation to institutions. As systems become more complex, they become less controlable. We may be entering a period of social disorder, in which public control will deteriorate and people become victims of random disturbances and chaotic events.

Moreover, the increasing specialization of public administration has made the governmental process more remote and incomprehensible. The lack of understanding of *how* government operates and ignorance *why* the state behaves as it does creates a credibility gap between the rulers and the ruled. This gap tends to separate the government from its constituency and threatens the very foundations of democratic politics. The evidence of the problem is manifested in the eroding confidence of leadership, mistrust of institutions, and disrespect for authority, all of which point to a crisis of political legitimacy.

Although this crisis is not worse than the social crisis already mentioned; it is more significant because it undermines the role of leadership in social change.

In the eyes of many people, the state has neither lived up to its principles nor responded adequately to the real needs of the community, thereby forfeiting the loyalty of its citizens.

The politics of compromise has not inspired respect for leadership in the more idealistic and vital parts of society, such as its youth. It often seems that problems are solved in inverse order of importance, so that the less significant the problem, the more time and effort spent on it. Crucial problems, on the contrary, sink the government into procrastination and immobilization.

As a result, the transition to an ecosociety appears almost impossible. The major shifts in the socio-economic process that the new society requires will need a strong political leadership that is lacking in liberal democracies. The energy necessary for the conversion and the accompanying strains on the system may prove too great to cope with by the present political institutions.

If authoritarian centralism is politically undesirable and local parochialism is realistically inadequate to solve complicated problems, then modern polities are in a precarious state indeed. The question remains: how can political leadership regain its moral authority and justify its legitimacy, at the same time as responsible citizenship recognizes its duties and exercises its rights?

Alternatives

Social Transformation Policies

The previous section outlined the factors which led to the problems an ecosociety will be called upon to solve. Diagnosing a cancerous growth of the techno-industrial complex, breakdown of the social system and crisis of confidence in political institutions, may be a pessimistic interpretation of historical trends and future expectations. Yet in dangerous times, political prudence demands that one err on the side of caution. If things are not as bad as all that, so much the better. What would be inexcusable is a *Panglossian* attitude which could lead to criminal negligence.

This section presents the conversion process by which the present consumer society could become a conserver one. Towards this end, the analysis proceeds in three steps: plan, policy, action. This logical sequence of decision-making considers the alternative courses of action for a society wanting to move from here to there. Since the polity acts as a receptor and transformer of social demands and supports into public policies; it has certain options and opportunities to channel inchoate social dissatisfaction into creative directions and positive goals. It is some of the most feasible of these roads to an ecosociety, that will now be discussed

Preparatory Activities

We begin with a look on social strategy, thus emphasizing the importance of public policy planning. Advanced societies are beginning to realize the necessity for a concerted postindustrial policy which will guide their transition to the next century. Although some are trying to move in this direction, there are many obstacles on the way.

One is the muddling-through tradition of *laissez-faire* government and another is the excesses of totalitarian *dirigism*. Although these are diametrically opposite reasons, they both stand in the way of proper public policy planning. Since both have failed miserably, they opened the way for a more eclectic and dialectic approach to complex social problem solving.

In order to change the anachronistic attitudes of either too much or too little government, public institutions must engage in value-forming and goal-setting, and lead society into a collective and purposeful action. Once this policy-making process is completed, then the final task of politics is to mobilize public support in implementing it. Moderate social planning, therefore, involves dialectical as well as rational processes.

Political Expediency and Feasibility

Unlike technology which progresses quite rapidly, ecology evolves very slowly. Social change runs in between, but with a reactive rather than proactive tempo. The resulting time-lags become critical when the accelerating change of technology is juxtaposed with the virtual absence of new discoveries in social innovation. The conservative inertia of social institutions creates an inverse relationship between political feasibility and magnitude of change. Accordingly, what is considered most feasible is incrementalism; while any serious consideration of sweeping innovations is called impractical idealism.

As is well known, political opportunism is oriented towards immediate and particular solutions. This orientation favors small or local problems and answers the pressures of particular interests. This phenomenon of time-discount which devaluates the future and emphasizes the here-and-now is characteristic of the politics of expediency.

It is not difficult to explain such orientation in liberal societies. Politicians who are elected for five year terms will not invest their time and energy in solving problems beyond their mandates, since they will not get credit for any successful solution and may be blamed for an investment whose pay-off is in another political generation. Their tendency is to postpone dealing with a problem and hope it becomes someone else's worry.

Yet the longer some problems are postponed, the more critical they become. Fast stop-gap solutions tend to exacerbate many problems in the long-run. Buying short-term relief by sacrificing long-term benefits is an understandable human weakness, but is nevertheless counterproductive as social policy. Many projections indicate that such short-sighted politics combined with exponential technological change can only lead to disaster.

Although politicians have consistently underestimated the repercussions of future changes, there are some hopeful signs that this might change. Some governments are moving from incremental postures to more planned policies, and the growth of planning staffs in public administration indicates some seriousness for strategic thinking.

A caveat here is that most planning so far is sectoral, carried out by separate departments and institutions with very little coordination. This kind of planning compounds problems by producing conflicting purposes and reenforcing functional and regional fragmentation. The most appropriate role of the polity in this respect is not only to encourage social planning, but we do so in a coordinated and systemic manner.

The Necessity for Planning

Rapid technological change creates personal insecurity and social instability which only strategic planning and political control can alleviate. Ephemeral or sectoral policies are inadequate in a fast-moving world because they are reactive and so become outdated before they are put into practice. Longer range rolling plans, on the contrary, are more anticipatory and deterrent so they both prevent and foresee potential problems. Such planning promotes more controlled change and creates more stable conditions for social dynamics. In order to decrease the risks of the unknown, the faster the rate of social change, the longer the range of policy planning necessary to deal with it.

Planning is not merely desirable but indispensable in the area of ecology. The only choice in this case is either to continue as before and let nature impose its inevitable limits by *force majeur*, or plan ahead to avoid a crisis by self-imposed controls. The first option relies on crisis management to carry the day and postpone the inevitable. The second option involves the art and science of sociopolitics: predicated on the assumption that we can best affect our collective future by timely action.

This attitude rejects both extremes of determinism and fatalism. In spite of the belief in causal and random events which combine to create our world of order and chaos, this position interjects human intentionality to complete the picture of reality. We posit the existence of a number of alternative possibilities which are open to human choice. As such, our will makes a difference in the scheme of things and the way it is exercised is crucial for its outcome.

Accordingly, humanity is partly responsible for its fate, and the best way to carry out such responsibility is through foresight and proaction. For that reason, integrated public policy planning must be carried out in several critical areas by assessing and auditing the repercussions of technological development upon society; reevaluating moral ideals and social norms to find out how they fit into the changing situation; and taking inventory of social institutions to see if they can handle the added burdens placed upon them.

Good policy planning is both pragmatic and idealistic. In order to avoid the mistake of simply extending the present into the future, it prepares to create the future by changing the present. Although it is based on present realities, it suggests how to redirect them to a more desirable future. This, as we shall see presently, not only involves social goals, but political power.

Social Goals and Priorities

Wishing for a particular future is not so much a matter of anticipation, but an act of inspiration and aspiration. It involves not only reason and foresight, but values, goals, choices, and decisions. Since policy options try to balance determined ends to selected means; planning must consider normative values, operational methods, and desired goals.

Policy-making is an exercise in normative planning and value-judgement aiming at decisions of both what can be done and what ought to be done. This process of combining the proper measures of feasibility and desirability is the essence of politics. Unfortunately, it is impossible to strike an exact balance in this ever changing world. Caught in this dilemma, some people resort to the extremes of either opportunism or fatalism.

Liberal leadership is traditionally pragmatic and opportunistic. It concerns itself with the present and simply tries to ride the prevailing wave to the future. This simple policy may have been good enough in older simpler times, but it is no longer adequate in this fast moving sophisticated world. Responsible leadership today requires more insight and foresight which can be converted into preventive and proactive policy. It involves searching for alternatives and finding potentials which then are put to the people for their opinion and selection.

For people to make veritable choices, they must be given various options and the consequences towards which they may lead. Finally, the government must take a stand and propose the direction it considers best. Yet most policy-makers fail to examine basic values, explain objectives, or assess consequences. Because of the multiplicity of issues, the volume of problems and the variety of values involved, political decision-making tends to be crisis-oriented, compromising, and amoral. It is this value-free orientation that is now called into question.

The dominant theme to emerge from the recent period of social introspection, has been a call for a systematic formulation of national priorities. It is increasingly recognized that rational public policy is impossible without clearly stated goals to guide social change. Establishing social priorities is first and foremost a political problem and so cannot be left to private initiative.

The power to select and implement the choices for the future is as awesome as the power to rule the present; both must be done by public institutions.

"*Gouverner c'est prévoir*" was never more true than it is now. Posing the right questions about the future and translating the answer of the community into policy is the measure of leadership, which contemporary government cannot afford not to exercise. Political leadership and policy planning are the necessary ingredients to mobilize and focus social energies towards collective goals, thereby reducing the great entropy losses of the present system.

Directing Social Change

Social change is directly proportional to social conflict, particularly in a complex and interdependent system. Setting new goals and planning a new society, reversing old priorities and traditions are therefore, bound to produce social conflict. The political confrontation that usually polarizes social conflict revolves around the *conservative-revisionist* axis. So demands for change always meet head-on the reaction of those who resist such change.

The *status quo* at any particular time is an intricate and dynamic process, rather than a simple stand-still. It reflects an equilibrium of opposing forces which have temporarily immobilized each other. Any change from such steady-state means a release of the locked-in energy of opposing views by some catalytic action. If the action is political, rather than physical, it will involve convincing the various vested interests that a particular change is preferable to the standing still. This conversion can only come about by either arguing that change promotes the self-interest of those who control the system, or persuading them that they have no choice in the matter. Political debate, pressure, and threat combine to prevail upon the powers that be to make the necessary compromises as the lesser evil, if not the higher good.

Any movement for change from the present consumer to the future conserver society will necessarily be opposed by vested interests everywhere. Since the implications of the ecosociety are not limited to conservation of resources, but spill-over beyond to socially responsible production, controlled consumption, equitable distribution, and wider participation; the resulting political conflict can be expected to be waged in many social arenas. Most people will be either for or against an ecosociety for different reasons. The resistance to change will not only come from producers but from consumers, not only from corporations but from unions, since both are locked in the same *status quo.*

Public opinion alone is not sufficiently enlightened or united to bring about an ecosociety. Although there is a heightened concern and deeper awareness of the limits of the consumer society among most people, only a small segment is organized enough to be politically relevant. Reevaluating life styles is a painful process, so the call to abandon the pursuit of affluence is not very popular. Many still refuse to believe the seriousness of the situation and change their ways. It took a long time and a lot of evidence for most people to accept that the Earth is round, so it may take as much time and energy to get a consensus that the world is finite. Programs and policies must, therefore, be well publicized by national campaigns of explanation and promotion.

Policy Alternatives

Now that the procedural aspects of policy planning have been covered, we move into the substantive side of policy itself. This involves the content of an *ecopolicy* in the broadest sense. Here we have to decide what the parameters of such policy and the variations within them are. Since we cannot be exhaustive in the coverage of all possible policy alternatives; two main ecopolicies of production and consumption control were chosen for discussion. We thereby concentrate on these two foci, and so span the range between minimal and maximal ecosocieties.

Essential Characteristics

Two broad criteria for evaluating public policy judge how well it fulfills human needs by reducing the threats of nature upon mankind and facilitating the resolution of conflicts within society; thereby improving the overall quality of life. It is our basic thesis here that an ecosociety provides the conditions in which this twin goal can be best attained. Given the necessity of prolonging the useful life of natural resources and artificial commodities; conservation policies extend in time and spread in space the optimal utilization of goods for human purposes.

The minimal conditions which conserver policies will have to meet are economism, futurism, and naturalism. These ensure that ecopolicies minimize waste, plan ahead, and take into account their impact upon nature. They thus postulate and promote an efficient attitude, a forward orientation, and an environmental respect, as the essential traits of desirable public policies.

Once a state adopts these three criteria for its policy-making, it will not be difficult to promulgate them in public. Most people are predisposed to follow government initiatives, if their leaders properly explain national priorities and thereby take the people into their confidence.

There is no doubt that a government which promotes efficiency and ecology can get wide public support. Unfortunately, such support is not so easy to get for proactive policies since this concept has not yet been sufficiently popularized. It is up to the leadership, however, to make it as acceptable to the public as the other two.

In any case, the political difficulty is not so much in the concepts, as in their translation into concrete policies. Efficiency is acceptable as long as it does not put people out of work; respect of nature is fine as long as everybody has fulfilled one's needs; and long-range planning is all right only after immediate necessities have been satisfied.

Production-control Emphasis

One of the two main operational options of an ecosociety is to control production so as to minimize waste and thereby conserve resources. The political obstacles to this option, as was mentioned, do not lie in its emphasis on efficient production, but in its translation and application. The principal worry of most people regarding this policy is that is might ruin the economy and lower the standard of living.

To alleviate such fears, the first thing ecopolicy proponents must do is differentiate between controlling and lowering production. It is not economic growth *per se*; but indiscriminate wild growth that is opposed. Such growth is not be confused with economic development, neither is the "standard of living" as it is presently measured be equated to the "quality of life" which ecosociety is promoting.

On the contrary, nature permitting, it is easier to raise the standard of living of the lowest segment of the population by increasing production than by forcing redistribution. The present rates of growth could continue until nobody suffers absolute deprivation any more. At the same time, however, there is no reason why such growth cannot be regulated to maximize efficiency. With appropriate technological innovations, waste and pollution can be decreased while production is increased. Thus, economic development can be made compatible with efficient production, environmental protection and resource conservation.

The main political question is who will effect such controls on production. Efficiency is not a monopoly of the state; the market also claims to maximize efficiency through competition. The alternative between socialist and capitalist options can be decided by a political compromise. A dialectical or pragmatic combination of the two positions that eschews dogmatism is not only most appropriate, but could result in the best of both worlds.

The present political and social climate does not allow any strong move towards greater state control. On the other hand, techno-economic necessities no longer permit a complete "free market" society. Consequently, an eclectic public policy means steering between *totalitarian* and *laissez-faire* solutions. Such middle course need not nationalize the means of production as the prerequisite of social control.

Private ownership can be made compatible with public responsibility through adequate political regulation of society's productive capacities. Social legislation and cost-internalization can attain the goals of the ecosociety, without undue dislocation or social conflict. To that end, the public could tighten social control over private decisions affecting large concentrations of labour and capital.

Consumption-regulation Emphasis

Production and consumption should be considered the two sides of the same coin, rather than independent processes. The alternatives between production and consumption policies are only in emphasis; they are not mutually exclusive. Their separation is for analytic purposes and not a realistic option.

In any case, it is easier to control production than consumption, because the economy is more amenable to legislation than is society as a whole. Social mores and traditions die hard. High consumption is by now such a way of life in hyperdeveloped societies that it would be politically impossible to persuade most people to become ascetics voluntarily. In an advanced stage of industrialization, it takes great power to reverse consumption patterns in a direct and immediate manner.

This does not mean that consumption cannot be influenced at all. A policy of responsible consumption can be sold to the electorate by emphasizing qualitative rather than quantitative consumption and popularizing tertiary or quaternary pursuits rather than primary or secondary commodities.

Since conservation is already a popular attitude in postindustrial societies, the next logical step is to adopt policies of responsible consumption which replace the conspicuous consumption of affluent hypertrophic societies. Such policies would limit the false freedom of the consumer to choose among a plethora of useless items, as well as curtail the licence of the producer to generate artificial demand for costly output.

Naturally, a significant change of consumption patterns requires a real change of social values which can only come about gradually and by a concerted effort of the major institutions of society. In some cases, there is more time to effect a gradual transition from material ostentation to healthy simplicity. But, apart from time, the main thing lacking is political will and social unity to carry out radical changes.

Politicians often underestimate their public though by assuming that most people are indulgent and irresponsible. As a result they tend to treat their constituents as pampered children who cannot understand the need for austerity in their consumption habits. This self-fulfilling prophesy perpetuates the myth of consumption and pre-empts any initiative to reform it. Nonetheless, it is a pessimistic assumption that can be reversed by careful reeducation campaigns that respect people as adults with whom it is worth discussing important public issues.

Distribution-equity Emphasis

Any political attempt to control the production and consumption processes would not only be incomplete but ineffective without some redistribution policy. The ecosociety's emphasis on redistribution is not only on grounds of moral equity, but also on political efficacy. People will accept greater sacrifices if they consider the goal not only necessary but fair. Common sense combined with a sense of justice is therefore, a very powerful political force. Production control and consumption rechanneling alone cannot create the powerful popular emotions that a more equitable distribution does. By adding "distributive justice" to its call for "responsible consumption" and "quality production," the polity could build up enough public support to make an ecosociety possible.

The redistribution issue, of course, is more politically explosive than either production or consumption problems. For that reason, it must be handled more carefully and in conjunction with the other two issues. Trying to minimize the ideologically charged connotations of redistribution, the leadership can promote the concept of community trusteeship of resources. The idea of man as the steward of nature justifies both production efficiency and consumption responsibility.

Sharing possessions fits in well with conserving resources and prolonging enjoyment. Such socialization combines renting or leasing programs; cooperative movements; communal living; condominium ownership; and time-sharing schemes. All these help distribute the wealth of society more equitably; and in doing so emphasize the collective enjoyment of goods and services, hence attenuating the excesses of exclusive consumption.

As in the case of production and consumption controls, distribution policies can be most effective without falling into either extreme capitalism or communism. What they do require is an emphasis on the public sector of the economy which produces social goods. This means concentrating social energies in: 1) reconstructing living spaces; 2) expanding public education; 3) improving community health; 4) developing public transport; 5) promoting collective recreation; and 6) spreading popular culture. All these things can be carried out by retraining and redeploying people in the new socio-economic system.

As we see later on when we go into the details of the policy content of these proposals, such activities can only be attempted by political institutions with the support of the social system. It is to this question of how popular support for the ecosociety can be generated that we turn.

Political Action

Here, we propose to deal with the political process necessary to bring about an ecosociety by presenting the general principles according to which social change of such magnitude can be effected. In liberal pluralistic societies, where governments have limited powers, certain methods are excluded and others avoided. This leaves a narrow range of procedural options within which political institutions can maneuver, so it is the best of these that are presented forthwith.

Conflict and Violence

The first and foremost option that is necessarily excluded from political activity is violence. Peaceful change is chosen not only on moral but on pragmatic grounds. Since politics is a civilized process of social change, it is particularly fitting for post-industrial societies where a violent revolution would be both impossible and undesirable. In such cases, prevailing socio-economic conditions make the chances for revolutionary change highly improbable, because there is neither mass support for it, nor sufficient power in anybody's hands to carry it out.

Moreover, in a sophisticated society, mass violence would be catastrophic. The fragility of complex systems makes them vulnerable to the slightest disturbance, so it would be foolhardy to gamble with any policy of violent change.

The most probable event that could produce a violent revolution in a post-industrial society would be precisely a failure to bring about an ecosociety by political means. Given the present symptoms and trends outlined in the first chapter, such eventuality cannot be excluded. Revolutions usually occur when a prolonged period of socio-economic growth is followed by a sharp reversal which frustrates the rising expectations of the people. It is such a dramatic reversal of fortune that can be expected in the aftermath of exponential growth; which only a gradual and planned redirection of social development can prevent.

In this sense, the political solutions proposed here not only make violence unnecessary, but provide the best means available to ensure that it does not happen. This is not to say that one can realistically expect the absence of any violence in such social context. The extent of violence is, however, inversely proportional to the success of politics. If the state or any other group uses violent means to effect or suppress change, it only means that politics failed its mission.

In the political arena, there is a difference between conflict and violence. Social conflict can be functional in a dynamic system, provided it is controlled and limited. Any political action assumes some conflict as a positive stimulus to social change. In that sense, politics can be a dangerous occupation, because it does not only resolve conflicts but generates them by focusing attention upon controversial agenda. At its worst, politics divides a community into factions and precipitates confrontations among them. For this reason, political conflict must remain within prescribed bounds and be carried out with the intention of being ultimately resolved by peaceful means.

A certain dynamic tension and social struggle helps solve problems by forcing those involved to reconsider their positions. Through political conflict, the various interest groups balance their relative weights to arrive at a collective compromise. In this sense, politics encourages individuals and groups to find mutually acceptable adjustments in a civil way. Political action aims to convince the establishment that a proposed change is either the right thing to do or it pays to do it. Thus by a combination of moral arguments and material rewards or deprivations, political activity manages social change.

In any case, the alternative to politics is either brute force and fanatic terrorism or irresponsible apathy and egoistic idiocy. Social conflict can be resolved either by political means or by various physical, chemical, and psychological techniques that may be invented to control human behavior. It is fortunate if a society can choose politics as a means to its ends.

Nevertheless, politics need not remain the lesser evil, but can become the greater good for social change. The political process can be improved and expanded so as to become a more effective instrument for creative innovation in public affairs. Indeed, political development may be measured by a society's ability to resolve its conflicts by itself without resort to violence; and so effect social change in an orderly manner.

In that respect, political underdevelopment may not coincide with its economic equivalent, since a poor society does not have to be either violent, dependent or repressed. Moreover, rapid industrialization tends to hinder political development. As indicated in the first chapter, consumer societies promote social passivity, which in itself indicates political maldevelopment. Thus an ecosociety will most likely exist in a politically developed country. These two go on in parallel, since ecopolitics can best bring about an ecosociety, and then further thrive in it.

Resistance to Change

Although a loyal public may be amenable to its political leadership, there still remain strong vested interests which can be counted on to resist radical social change. Powerful sectoral organizations accept certain changes only if they benefit from them. From their point of view, the common good is dangerous because it does not pay special attention to their particular interests. Any drastic shifts of power could mean a loss of their relative, if not absolute, position.

The most powerful opposition to the ecosociety is not expected from individuals *per se,* but from organized groups whose privileges would suffer in a social restructuring. Where the nature of the polity militates against a strong centralized leadership, promoting an ecosociety, is a delicate task so as not to crystalize undue opposition. Every step could only be taken after adequate consultation and accommodation with the established power centers.

As mentioned previously, political power is usually diffused both regionally and functionally.

Regional breakdown is primarily institutionalized in the geopolitical divisions of the country; wherein the central government can be considered a cooperative organization for territorial coordination. Developing an ecosociety will necessarily mean overcoming regional opposition and local resistance. An overall social policy can then be successful only with the cooperation of the various regional interests. For that reason, further consultative mechanisms must be developed for consensus-building by joint intergovernmental bodies.

On the functional level, special attention should be given to both business and syndicates, since they can be initially expected to oppose the ecosociety. It is ironic that these two adversaries could be found on the same side on this issue. Such disparate organizations as manufacturers associations, chambers of commerce, as well as professional societies and labor unions, would most likely interpret an ecosociety negatively at first.

In order to overcome such potential concerted opposition, the political leadership would have to convince the elites of these organizations that an ecosociety is not only unavoidable but that with sufficient cooperation it would turn out to the benefit of all. The success of this movement is essential in order to ensure peaceful and orderly change. It is not enough for the polity to disseminate information before major policy changes, it must prepare the ground long before by continuing discussion and consultation on all contentious issues.

In this case, trilateral talks (governments, employers and employees) could be instituted on a permanent basis. For this purpose, a consultative forum should be established to facilitate exchange of views among the representatives of the main interest groups. Open discussions elucidate the issues at stake and attempt to reach a consensus on collective orientations. Such public forum would consider the impact of the ecosociety on various social groups and recommend ways of sharing its costs and benefits equitably.

By promoting constructive public debate, we can forestall conflict-oriented behavior among various interest groups. In favoring functional adjustment, social communication and consensus-building strategies, the polity could achieve its objectives with a minimum of conflict.

Citizen Participation

Resistance to social change does not come only from vested interests, but also from the mental inertia that has dulled most people's spirit. It is the habit of passivity and apathy in the silent majority that allows vocal minorities to set the political agenda. In order for special limited interests to loosen their hold over society, more people must enter the political arena and get involved in public affairs.

As may be expected, ecopolicies will be opposed in some quarters, so broadening the active base of support is imperative. If people are shaken from their lethargy, they will participate in the significant issues which concern them. Elections are not be the beginning and end of citizenship duty, but only one of its formalities. True democracy requires citizens with a continuous commitment to public affairs, something that is possible with increasing education and leisure.

It is now becoming quite clear that *participatory democracy* is emerging as one of the great themes of our times. There is already enough evidence to suggest that we are entering into a new era in which more individuals and groups are demanding a voice in the policy-making process. The emerging politics of involvement make for more visible issues that draw people into the public arena. This is particularly so for the young, the intelligent, and the minorities, who are no longer content to accept decisions made by remote authorities. Demands for participation in decision-making are made not only in the political realm, but also in every social context: schools, unions; corporations, and families. According to these indices, it is hopeful that the trends of greater involvement will continue to promote social change leading towards an ecosociety.

From the above indicators, it could be that we are witnessing a significant change of our political culture. The notion of authority is shifting from a certain source to a particular process. Policies are no longer regarded as legitimate simply because they emanate from an authoritative center. An increasing segment of the population only accepts decisions in the formulation of which it has participated. Policies are, therefore, acceptable only when they take into account the consequences they have upon society and nature, as well as when they are made by those who will be affected by their impact. Social change can no longer be legitimated unless it is reached through public participation and community involvement.

Political initiatives

Politics competes with many other human activities. Given the limited time and energy people have, it is usually at the bottom of most people's priorities. In order to reverse this condition, popular interest in public affairs must be rekindled. If politics is not to be left to fringe groups of activists, on the one hand, and powerful elites, on the other; political institutions must not only welcome broad participation, but mobilize political action. Only a combination of the people and their representatives can counter the reaction of vested interests and the irresponsibility of self-appointed saviours.

Increased *politicization*, if it takes place haphazardly can get out of control and result in chaos where everyone is fighting everyone else. It is the duty of the political institutions to see that such politicization is constructive rather than destructive, civil rather than barbaric. In this task, the polity is in the best position to guide the political development of a country and channel the energies of the most active people into positive directions.

Social change could come about by allocating resources to local groups that show their willingness to promote socially useful and viable projects. The contact between people and their government can be increased by exchanging information and proposals. The best way for the polity to influence public opinion is by making the public participate in policy-making. It is upon such mutual exchange of influence and consultation that a consensus as to both goals and means of attaining them can be built.

The creative art of *consensus-building* is the primary act of citizenship. It is the loftiest occupation of the free person; the most relevant activity that advanced people are seeking. As such, it is the process by which political conflict is transformed into social cooperation. This transformation can only be achieved by free and secure people, whose position and opinion are fully respected and taken into account.

Political leadership can play a crucial part in raising the level of public discussion. In this context, leaders act as guidance counsellors or social animators, explaining to people the consequences of their actions and presenting alternatives so that citizens can decide intelligently. This means that the aimless drifting of current politics could acquire a definite orientation by the mutual cooperation of prudent leadership and responsible citizenship.

The Optimal Ecosociety
Preferable Future Scenario

This section ends the chapter by presenting the main characteristics of an ecosociety at the golden mean of the conservation range. As the previous section outlined the various policy options open to a government regarding ecosociety, this one combines the salient points of these options to form an *eclectic ecosociety model* which is both feasible and desirable.

This optimal model is presented by analyzing three important areas essential in identifying any society: that is, geopolitical culture, socioeconomic structure, and public institutions. In order to move from the present consumer society to a desired conserver one, we must change to some extent *value-systems*, directly related to *social structures*, both of which support *political institutions*. Even if such an optimal society cannot be attained in this century, it can serve as the ultimate objective orienting public policy.

Political Culture

Underlying any human society is a culture or way of life that animates collective behavior. Social culture is manifested in values that motivate action, as well as in methods that people utilize to attain these values. Here, of course, we cannot go into the whole gamut of cultural traits of an ecosociety. The aim is, rather, to determine the political aspects of an ecoculture. This means considering the constitutional framework within which society makes collective decisions. The procedural side of political culture is necessarily related to the substantive side of the social culture. Political form is, therefore, tied to the social content, both of which make an ideology. We can, thus, speak of an *eco-ideology* to describe the most significant public values of the ecosociety.

In order to develop and maintain an ecosociety, one must generate an ideology that legitimizes and justifies such social system. New value priorities and political symbols must be created to attract people's loyalties and appeal to their better sense. In particular, one needs a new *cooperative morality* to guide social relations and replace the *competitive ethos* of the consumer society. In order to divert energy from the aimless growth of material economy, we must develop a program with *stated objectives* and *explicit strategies*. These, then, are the areas to be covered.

Value-Orientation

Social systems, not only embody, depend upon and preserve values, but also serve as vehicles to confirm and implement value changes. In this respect, *political values* take on transcendental significance, because they can distort, facilitate, or impede the capacity to make collective choices. No single value, regardless of its virtue, can affect social issues, unless a sufficient number of people share it. Through these shared values, people can arrive more easily at consensus and minimize coercion and violence. Infusing an ideological or value-system orientation to a social movement makes it easier to capture the imagination of people and coalesce them into action. The force of an *ideology* is therefore very important for social change.

It is unfortunate that ideological evolution lags behind technological development. While we are approaching the twenty-first century in scientific innovations, we are still encrusted in nineteenth century ideological dogmas. The concept of an ecosociety can only develop together with an ideology of the future. The new ideology must modify man's adolescent drive to dominate nature with a more mature appreciation that humanity is only part of the nature. In order to resolve the value-dissonance of rampant technology, we need a holistic ethic of socio-natural dynamics.

Human development requires the ability to transcend the limitations of selfishness and loneliness. Future ideals would have to temper the belief in some inalienable rights inherent to individuals with equivalent duties to the social system as well as their natural environment. The present focus on personal achievement should be supplemented by an emphasis on collective actualization. Individual independence should be balanced with social interdependence, competition with collaboration, and ownership with trusteeship. In general, cultural development should follow natural evolution which moves from *atomic* to *organic* systems.

The ideology of an ecosociety will have to involve with a new *social contract* whose aim is to :

1) humanize science by discovering what is empirically good for mankind;
2) socialize economics by making it a true art of ecosystem management;
3) functionalize institutions by serving human purposes, needs and values;
4) enlighten education by evolving a permanent activity of social learning.

These imperatives would veer society away from acquisitive consumption to enjoyable conservation, from technical virtuosity to natural simplicity, and from quantitative growth to qualitative excellence. Ultimately, it will give people a reason for living at peace within themselves and among their neighbors, as well as in harmony with nature. It is mainly up to cultural institutions to develop such new ideology which legitimizes and popularizes these ecological values.

Social-Health and Life-Quality

Just as the notion of health is a biological norm, *social health* and *quality of life* could become normative standards for society. The concept of health could be expanded to describe a state of physical, psychological, and social *well-being*, and not merely the absence of some identifiable disease or infirmity. Humans are organisms having extremely precise physiological, biological and mental attributes. Although they are quite malleable, there are limits beyond which the price of adjustment may be the loss of humanity. Accelerated change, restricted space, extended temperature or pressure variations, not to speak of undernourishment or malnutrition, disturb normal metabolism and should be avoided.

The life-sciences have by now arrived at certain conditions in which human beings are considered healthy. These include: 1) caloric intake; 2) physical activity; 3) mental stimulation; and 4) clement environment. A healthy organism must receive the proper nutrients of matter, energy, and information in order to function adequately. This means, one should be able to operate in such a way as to exercise all of one's faculties. Basic to human survival, then, is sufficient mental and physical activity. Not being able to do so, for any reason, is *pathological*, and spells immediate malfunction and eventual death.

Whatever else an ecosociety may do, it provides people with the conditions and facilities for a healthy life. This assumes that postindustrial systems have sufficient resources to satisfy the basic needs of their people without forcing them to compete for the necessities of life. This assumption, of course, excludes the insatiable demands created by consumerism in order to keep the industrial economy growing. The values of the ecosociety thereby shift from the material overconsumption which creates obese, inactive, neurotic, and unhappy people, to those human needs that can be optimally fulfilled. Fortunately, these activities do not require large inputs of depletable resources. Better food, education, artistic expression, athletics, and enjoyment of nature, are all possible with a modicum of material production and leisure time. It is these activities that promote health and measure the quality of life.

To that end, the proposed ecosociety must develop a proper system of *social indicators* which relate individual to social health. The present economic indicators and especially the GNP index are misleading measures of the quality of life. Moreover, such economic orientation emphasizes subjective desires and raises expectations that can never be fulfilled for most people. Since these material demands cannot be met, they must be deflected to realistic needs.

The ecosociety will develop *social standards* of public health and welfare and try to maximize them in a systematic way. In this respect, the United Nations Human Development Index is a good start. Improving such HDI, together with a Social Development Index will go a long way to measuring holistic development, rather than merely economic growth.

Permanent Education

In order to change social values, the community must undertake the re-education of its citizens. Since most societies have control over education; it is their right and duty to engage in broadly educational activities in economic, cultural and political issues. In periods of rapid change, education becomes a life-long process of adjustment and at the same time the main carrier of change.

Building up an ecosociety requires a sustained effort of adult re-education to get people to change their wasteful and polluting ways and cure them of their "infernal innocence" which is destroying both nature and culture. One major sign of social decay is the irrelevance of formal education in propagating new cultural values and ideals. This gap between traditional values, which are disfunctional or outdated, and future values, which are not yet formulated or promulgated, can only be filled by a bold shift in the educational establishment.

Education, in the broadest sense, may well become the central business of society by the next generation, when half the population may be attending some kind of school at any particular time. The old-fashioned idea, that there is a time for learning and a time for doing, is being replaced by permanent education concurrently with working experience. Thus, the society's role in this process of continuous education, as in economics, can no longer be *laissez-faire*. The two areas are fusing, not only because the state provides trained manpower for the economy, but also because control of education indirectly determines social priorities.

Proper training increases the worker's commitment and efficiency, at the same time as it increases concerns and pressures for decision-making in production. Many studies have shown that there is a striking correlation between education and participation. Less educated people are more submissive to authoritarian structures; whereas more educated people are less dependent and so demand to be treated with greater respect and consideration. At the same time, the more educated are less fanatical and do not believe in radical solutions and bloated promises.

In general, education makes better citizens by heightening civic consciousness and social concern. Educated persons are more realistic and understanding of the problems facing them. Through permanent education, people are continuously sensitized to the changing constraints on their behavior. Education loosens ingrained habits and develops an open receptivity for new values and actions. Unless such educational transformation is successful, coercion becomes the only alternative to social change.

Systemic-Entropy and Steady-State

The concept of health underlies a notion of homeo-stasis or dynamic equilibrium between the various elements of a system and its environment. On the contrary, disease implies some imbalance or instability either within the organism or between it and the rest of nature. This balance is dynamic because it is constantly changing, but, at the same time, it does so in an orderly way.

A particular instance of steady-state is manifested in natural growth, which generally goes through three stages:

1) the slow initial growth of the developing system;
2) the takeoff stage of accelerated exponential growth;
3) the decelerated linear stability of maturity.

Social systems go through this pattern of sigmoid development. If such analogy between organic and social systems is accepted, it would seem that advanced societies are completing their second stage of development and every indication leads us to believe that they are presently entering the third. Either we adopt this model and prepare to transform our physical cellular growth into a psycho-social development, or we will follow the road to temporary gigantism and ultimate collapse.

The inevitability of slowdown in physical growth is tied to the principle of universal *entropy*. As everything else, individual and social life are losing the fight against the natural forces of entropy. We combat entropy by building islands of law and order in a sea of deterioration and enervation. Life's desire for *syntropy* is labeled as "good," whereas its opposite process of entropy leading to death is considered as "bad." But, as it is individually desirable to prolong life and delay death, so it is naturally imperative to perpetuate species and preserve the ecosystem balance, in spite of the fate of individuals.

These contradictory objectives may be accommodated by a responsible social policy which prolongs life by minimizing the waste of energy and promoting a higher level of dynamic equilibrium. A *syntropic society* strengthens social-bonding among its individuals and groups, thus increasing the integration of its systems. By definition, this society attains its mature stage of organic growth when material expansion gives way to spiritual development. The extroversion of adolescent growth then becomes the introspection of the *mature society*.

When we recognize that culture must coexist with nature, we then accept the notion of *ecobalance* and social health as basic standards of public policy. The new values of life-quality and steady-state divert attention from the problems of production and consumption to those of distribution. As demands on nature decrease, our relations to each other become paramount. The exhaustive producer and the passive consumer of modern society becomes the active participants of social life in the ecosociety. The consumer-spectator culture of the present can then be replaced by the conserver-animator society of the future.

Socio-Economic Structure

Along with the changes in cultural values, the ecosociety also affects the economic structures of society. The relationship between society and economy is reflected in the technological ethic of the modern world which espouses the principle that anything technically possible must also be socially desirable. This ethic, along with that of perpetual growth, has to be demoted in the value priorities of an ecosociety.

Such relocation of *techno-economic values* necessarily affects attitudes towards work and property. Economic activity and private ownership have to be modified to fit the new values of social-health and steady state. These relationships between private economic activities and public affairs should now be investigated.

Work and Leisure

It is already evident that the protestant work ethic is undergoing a serious transformation in the postindustrial era. A more educated and affluent labor force is increasingly unwilling to work in degrading and routine jobs. A younger and more idealistic generation demands more meaningful work which puts its talents into social service as well as private profit. People realize that the more one works for money, the less time one has to enjoy its rewards; and the more goods one can buy, the less able one is to use them. Given this new attitude towards work and play, the ecosociety can easily channel it towards its social priorities and utilize it to strengthen its values.

An ecosociety develops the art and science of *ergonomics* in order to make work more interesting and agreeable to its people and so bring it closer to leisure activities. Unlike industry, ergonomy adjusts work to human needs. Ergonomics not only saves effort and minimizes waste, but does so without mechanizing and taylorizing the worker into smaller and simpler compartments.

When work is no longer necessary for survival and subsistence, it becomes sufficiently pleasant to attract people by presenting challenging and rewarding things for them to do. As more and more of the routine and boring tasks are automated, human work can become more creative and free. As this happens, people rediscover the joy of work. Indolence is a pathological symptom of forced labor and can be minimized when work becomes voluntary, educational, interesting and personalized, in short, when it is considered worthwhile. Consequently, work improves in efficiency, not only by technological innovations, but by better utilization of human capabilities which are now so tragically wasted.

Activity and Welfare

Individual and collective health, as we saw, requires the proper balance between production and consumption, work and play. Yet, an affluent society is characterized by its high consumption and low participation. It is this unhealthy imbalance that the ecosociety corrects. The curse of advanced techno-economies is that they produce chronic *anergy*, which in turn creates marginal and unwanted people. A growing underclass of humanity or lumpen proletariat, thus, becomes superfluous and parasitic upon the rest of society, which then must develop various subsistence schemes to support it.

Instead of unemployment insurance and welfare services, all people should have a chance to earn an income so that they are not stigmatized as second-class citizens. Self-respect requires the reciprocation of services. An ecosociety reverses the trend which reduces mankind to an anachronistic vestige of history, by assuring every person suitable employment. It would be the duty of the ecosociety to match everyone with some useful employment, balancing contributive and distributive justice.

People should be given a chance to work together, to plan and act in concert, and do something meaningful beyond the money-making jobs of present-day life. Community work makes people feel needed and responsible. As a social animal, man wants to belong to something larger than himself and fulfill more than private needs. In this respect cooperative work and team effort give particular psychological satisfaction that makes up for any physical inconvenience. The sense of involvement in some meaningful work and the pride of participating in decision-making is thus more important than the end-product of these activities.

People must make an effort to attain their values; they do not appreciate what they get for free. Humans tend to rise up to meet their challenges and overcome adversity, but sink to torpidity in comfortable and easy lives. It is for this reason that the hedonism of the consumer society leads to sterility, boredom, and decadence. The fewer material comforts of the ecosociety will, therefore, revitalize humanity as well as economy. A new social consciousness will then go beyond the welfare state into the healthy community.

In order to tap human energies into creative and dynamic areas, there has to be a high degree of sociocybernetics. This control, however, need not be forced upon people from above. Highly educated and energetic citizens cannot be manipulated. Mature persons are asked not ordered, convinced not commanded, consulted not forced. As such, their incentives are more sophisticated than simple material payments, but include social and psychological rewards which are both more economic and satisfying.

Private Property and Enterprise

As work in the ecosociety is synergistic, so property is functional. As productive activities become more social and cooperative, their rewards cannot remain so exclusive as private property. This does not mean that ownership is abolished or property expropriated, but, rather, that such relations lose their social relevance. Education and information become much more valuable commodities than real estate. A shift from the static spatial aspects of value towards more dynamic functional aspects therefore, becomes inevitable. Functional socialization will separate title from control of property. Changing the formal structure of ownership not only is superfluous but counterproductive. As long as society controls the use of private property, be it material or intellectual, its formal ownership can remain in the hands or minds of individuals.

The crucial element here is, of course, *social control*, especially in cases where property is accumulated in great quantities, and so becomes politically oppressive. Any control of production and consumption, let alone distribution, necessarily affects property. An ecosociety cannot allow private enterprise to decide major public priorities. Private corporations may be left to their own devices as long as they play by the rules of society and do not impose external costs upon others. Business must still make a reasonable profits, but only if its products and services are deemed at least socially harmless, if not positively useful.

Private initiative should be rewarded when it promotes social as well as personal goals. What is needed is more social entrepreneurship to turn future benefits into present investments. Profit is quite appropriate when it acts as an incentive for social benefactors. Business should, therefore, be encouraged to find ways to make a profit by conserving non-renewable resources and eliminating pollution.

Corporate responsibility, however, means that profit is not the sole consideration and reward for private enterprise. For social purposes to be respected by private decision-makers, the representatives of various groups must participate in the policies of corporations. This means that producers, consumers, and distributors, must supplement the investors and executives in the control of business. Employees, buyers, sellers, and governments should also become shareholders with an active voice in the board of directors. A participatory economy becomes the best complement to a participatory polity.

The Public Sector

In spite of any democratization of private enterprise, there still remains the problem of cooperation and coordination of the various sectors of the economy to fit within the overall system. Unless one still believes in the "invisible hand," there is no feasible way of regulating private behavior other than public control. Only political institutions are responsible for social development in all its aspects. Group interests must, therefore, accept subordination to the common good. Since only a central government can oversee and appreciate the total picture, any systemic planning must be centrally coordinated.

This, of course, does not mean totalitarian centralization. Within the general and flexible guidelines set by the state, private or local groups can make decisions as to the application of these guidelines in each particular case or local instance. Here, public policy can best influence private activity by combining the techniques of subsidy, regulation and manipulation, more effectively than by negative controls and sanctions.

According to the principle of subsidiarity, public institutions should undertake to do only things that private initiative cannot or will not do. Since it is always the people who pay for the services provided to them, social tasks should be assigned from lower to higher bodies on the basis of their functional efficiency and effectiveness.

The economy of an ecosociety is neither restrictive nor recessive, but rechanneled towards social development and cooperative distribution of the commonwealth. The principle of steady-state requires that development go on continuously and steadily, without extremely disturbing vacillations. To ensure social stability, the public sector should balance the private, so that it can guarantee a modicum quality of life, beyond which private enterprise can thrive unimpaired.

There is neither economic nor political reason why a healthy balance could not be attained between the public and private sectors of society. In this way, the discretionary income of private citizens and corporations would complement their public contributions in promoting social spending and investing policies.

Public Institutions

Having covered the cultural and economic aspects of ecopolitics; we now present some specific public functions relating to these aspects. Since the values and actions of a society are reflected in the public institutions that carry them out, the most significant institutionalized activities of the ecosociety will be technological evaluation, knowledge communication, and political organization. Let's discuss each one in turn.

Technological Assessment

It is imperative that the government of an ecosociety channel the flood of technological applications into a manageable stream, thereby ensuring that no new development is let loose upon society unless it is carefully examined. The techno-economic approach, whose credo is that "whatever can be made and sold should be manufactured and marketed," will then be replaced by a socio-political approach emphasizing manifest need as determined by public institutions.

Social control of technology means that society determines:

1) side-effects or byproducts of any new invention;
2) social changes necessary to accommodate such development;
3) net advantages after all social costs have been calculated.

Of course, such cost-benefit accounting cannot be very accurate since it is always based on incomplete information, but the principle is there to be followed as much as practically possible.

An ecosociety is not anti-technological. On the contrary, only sophisticated technology can get us out of the present predicament. Better, rather than bigger technology is needed to clean the environment, conserve resources, and alleviate poverty. Instead of more inventions of new gadgets for private consumption, research and development can concentrate in ameliorating the massive problems that affect society as a whole.

Moreover, scientific research could focus on technical innovations to improve social institutions, values, and behavior. Since our basic problems are not so much technological as political, their solution depends above all on political will. Instead of being an independent variable, technology becomes subordinated to the new social purpose and creativity. To this end, the public should ensure that technology is put in the service of society and science is tamed to the will of humanity.

Communication of Information

Non-violent social change necessarily depend upon convincing people of the desirability and necessity of innovation. Persuading rather than forcing people to change their ways depends upon the capacity to impart information. The role of the mass media in this highly political process of changing minds is indispensable, because it comprises the communication channels can carry messages from and to the public.

Political control of communications can be used to shape public opinion in favor of an ecosociety. The role of broadcasting in this process of consensus-building is crucial. As the mass media has been responsible in promoting consumerism, so it could become the messenger for conservationism. The well-known influence of advertising can then be used to disseminate the new eco-ideals.

For this purpose, some constraint should be imposed upon the mass-media. Commercial advertising must be controlled to ensure responsible consumption. The government, moreover, could go further to improve the quality of radio and television programming. Unfortunately, television viewing has been shown to be inversely correlated with education and politicization. The most avid television fans are the least educated and most apathetic part of the population. This explains the low quality and deadening effect of the programs which aim to please the lowest common denominator of their audience. To change this abominable situation, the broadcasters must be pressured to minimize escapist entertainment and maximize informative programming.

At the same time the veil of secrecy should be lifted from political communication. Freedom of information acts already began this process, whereby state plans and intentions are widely scrutinized and publicized in order to encourage public debate. If people are to exercise real and effective choices, they must be given all available facts and alternatives from which to choose. Unless special cases clearly prove to the contrary, public disclosure should become the norm of government accountability.

Political Organization

The failure of legitimacy and authority in public institutions is one of the major causes of the internal disintegration of societies. The respect that people accord their institutions diminishes along several dimensions, of which increasing size and disparity of the constituents is one. The growth of institutions tends to belittle men who feel powerless in the face of these leviathans. This growth, along with the accompanying centralization of decision-making, makes people feel like marginal appendages to mechanical monoliths.

According to the structural principle of form, there is a maximum size for any system before it collapses from its own weight. The mythology of techno-economics which equates big with good and relates size with efficiency may be true up to a point. In many areas, however, it has by now surpassed the limits of human tolerance. Social scientists have come to recognize that there are narrow ranges to the size and composition of social organization. It has been found that seven hundred people is the upper limit of personal interaction. This datum, combined with the upper limit of information that a person can handle at any time, would bring the size of the optimal community not much higher than the ideal *Platonic polis* of about 5000 voting citizens. This, then, should be the core unit of ecopolitics in a human scale.

For an ecosociety to become politically acceptable, it must provide people with a strong community organization. The best incentive to get people to consume less is to offer them an alternative mode of self-expression. In order to take away man's fake freedom as "king of the supermarket," we should replace it with the real freedom to participate in shaping the future.

People must become actively involved in every facet of their lives through face-to-face group interaction. Only local groups allow such informal exchange of views that is indispensable to decision-making. For that reason, the ecosociety promotes decentralization of government and devolution of power to the community level, wherein individuals get a greater sense of responsibility and self-determination.

The function of the state in this operation would be to consent to the necessary constitutional changes increasing local jurisdiction. Accordingly, each government level should have the necessary powers to do whatever needs to be done at that level and no more. The ecosociety can be planned and coordinated centrally, but applied and decided upon locally.

The Conserver Polity

It cannot be overemphasized that people rethink their cultural values and reorganize their political structures. To attain the goals of social change, certain sacrifices are inevitable which only highly motivated people can stand. Only societies blessed with extraordinary political leadership, strong public institutions, and responsive civic conscience can survive the transitory shocks from prodigality to frugality. In this case, public authority goes together with deep political loyalty and strong community identity.

It takes a dynamic and popular government to propose difficult goals and mobilize public support for them. Yet, most political institutions are devoid of a coherent message that fires the imagination of the people. Unfortunately, many countries clearly lack the legitimate authority to articulate social values; it is difficult to reach a shared image or collective goals.

In the dawn of the post-industrial age, however, political ideals and actions cannot be simply handed down from some high authority. Humanistic values are formulated by consensus among various social sectors and groups. Influence is multidirectional between public and private, local and national institutions. Hierarchical control structures share their power with egalitarian cooperative networks. The movement of the times is clearly a liberation from traditional constraints and loosening of vertical relations. Political authority is, therefore, redirected and redefined in functional terms.

The primary justification for government is serving collective human needs, rather than fulfilling individual desires or group interests. Public institutions and their policies must solve social problems and produce collective goods. Responsible leadership is accordingly accountable to popular wants, without slavishly following them.

At the same time, people ought to defer to their leaders, without blindly obeying everything they say. Such two-way communication and appreciation brings about mutual influence and respect. Only through this kind of political interaction can a new society that is both ecologic and democratic develop and avoid the double pitfalls of anarchism or totalitarianism.

CHAPTER FOUR

Gaiapolitics

The Ecosociety in a Turbulent World

Although the plight of the world could be overdramatized, it is better to err on the side of caution. From the hindsight of almost half a century, we can say that the world situation has improved in some respects and deteriorated in others. The nuclear threat has been resolved by the demise of the Soviet Union and its Eastern Bloc; but other problems have worsened. Apart from the end of the cold war and the reversal of its arms race; the environment, population, and development issues are still with us more than ever. It is, therefore, prudent not to rest on our laurels, but turn our attention to the looming global problems which threaten the planet.

It is not known how long we have to reverse the catastrophic trends that lead to the precipice. The danger is that parochial and ephemeral concerns focus on the here and now and discount the whole picture in the long run. This is especially so for people living in postindustrial societies whose relative insulation from the worst aspects of the Earth's deterioration gives them a false sense of security. This attitude must be dispelled, first by consciousness raising, then by political action.

The thesis of this chapter on *Gaiapolitics* is that the planet is a whole Earth *ecosphere* which is now coextensive with a single World *sociosystem*: *Gaia* and *Ecumene* have become coterminous. This development means that we cannot solve global problems separately and temporarily. Creating an ecosociety in postindustrial countries, will require both internal and external considerations. In many respects the latter are more important and intractable than the former.

This chapter is also divided into three sections covering the relevant inputs to the world system; an ecosociety's response to them; and the preferred outcome of the whole process. We first analyze the present macropolitical situation of the world and the trends to which it is prone in the foreseeable future; then, we put forth the major alternative foreign policies open to an ecosocial state; and finally complete the chapter by prescribing the conditions for and optimal ecoworld.

Parameters

Environmental Inputs to the World System

The success of an ecosociety in one country obviously depends to a large extent on what happens to the rest of the world. For this reason, we look into these external constraints that delimit one's freedom of action in certain directions. These constraints are manifested in macrohistorical forces over which no one has much influence. The two most contradictory of these forces are the megatrends towards greater economic interdependence and, at the same time, greater political independence. Let us deal with these two forces which divide and unite the world simultaneously, thereby, setting up the context to which every country must necessarily adapt.

Transnational Interdependence

Perhaps the most visible phenomenon of contemporary international life is the increasing interdependence among the various parts of the global system. The world is becoming more complicated and interwoven. Contacts and connections are multiplying, so that whatever happens in one part affects the others. This social development has a critical impact upon the natural environment for the reasons presented below.

Technological Modernization

The modern world is characterized by rapid and radical change in all areas of human activity. This change is primarily the result of spreading western science and values throughout the planet. The success of technology in bestowing wealth and power to its possessors has attracted everyone to its cause. Industrialization has become the goal of all preindustrial countries and economic growth has been raised to a universal panacea. Increasing the material production and consumption of their people is now the declared policy of governments everywhere. *Economic development* at all speed and cost has become the ideology, if not religion of the modern world.

In such feverish climate, any talk of ecological constraint is anathema. As the recent United Nations Conference on the Environment and Development showed, nobody wants to sacrifice one's own development for the sake of everybody's environment. On the contrary, economic growth is considered the palliative that will cure all the ills of the world, most of which were caused precisely by economic growth.

The two well-known by-products of industrialization —environmental pollution and resource depletion— do not seem to worry many governments in their rush to industrialize their societies. By creating material abundance, they hope to resolve another problem caused by western science: that is, overpopulation. The accompanying ills of the population explosion —congestion, malnutrition, poverty— are slated for solution by massive doses of industrialization. Such growth is supposed to solve both demographic and ecologic problems, thus, fulfilling the rising expectations of people everywhere.

Meanwhile, spreading westernization creates poor carbon copies of industrial societies throughout the world. Indiscriminate transplanting of technology and exporting of capital disturbs the global ecosystem, at the same time as it corrupts its local cultures Wherever industrialization takes place, it exacerbates the maldistribution of income by creating small enclaves of rich westernized elites in the midst of abject misery.

Even worse than the general scarcity and the maldistribution of wealth created by rapid growth, there is the diminishing marginal utility of people, millions of whom find themselves idle and useless in a mechanical society that would rather see them disappear. Not only does modernization result in a deteriorating environment and depleting resources, but it inflates the number of people and devalues their individual worth.

Finally, the political repercussions of such rapid social change soon manifest themselves in civil strife, political instability, violent confrontations, and community disintegration. The differential growth rates of innovation and population end up in increasing demands both on nature and culture, thus, heightening political pressures and conflicts, both within societies and the world at large.

Transnational Corporations

The most important carrier of technological modernization is international trade and commerce. Global business and financial institutions transcend political boundaries to spread a homogenized culture of material production and mass consumption throughout the world. Trans-National Corporations (TNCs) disseminate their work ethos wherever they operate, and so integrate the international economy into an interdependent network. The global corporation utilizes the technology of one country, the capital of another, the labour of a third, the resources of a fourth, and sells its products to a fifth. This creates a tremendous web of coordinated activities involving a multiplicity of public and private institutions.

These techno-economic developments deeply affect the geo-political structure of the world. The internationalization of the market challenges the predominance of sovereign states as the traditional protagonists in the world stage. Since the territorial institution of the national state intersects the functional organization of the transnational corporation, it results in a complex politico-economic matrix. The two institutions compete for the allocation of resources, investments and labor, as well as the essence, timing and location of decision-making. Heavy trends indicate that this competition favors *transnationalism*, reflected in the growth rate of TNCs which far exceeds that of nation-states. This is, of course, particularly true of the poor and weak states which form the majority of the world and are fast losing control of their territories.

The dominant creed of transnationalism is that nationalism, once the midwife of the industrial revolution, has now become the chief culprit to economic development and social progress. Transnationalists put great energy into packaging and marketing a new gospel of peace and plenty. Their leadership is trying to create public acceptance of this cosmopolitan creed as the most effective and rational force to develop and distribute the resources of the world.

This claim to political legitimacy not only runs counter to the national interests of many countries, but challenges the values and goals of the ecological movement. The corporation's inherent tendency to maximize profits by mass-production and technological efficiency clashes with the desire to limit material growth and preserve nature.

Furthermore, corporate centralization and hierarchy focuses all significant policy-making in metropolitan headquarters, while delegating to the periphery the role of "hewers of wood and drawers of water." These inequalities promote unbalanced economic growth and impede stable political and social development, as well as stifle local initiative and perpetuate relations of exploitation and overdependence.

Global Integration

The growth of transnationals has been accompanied by the multiplication of many other institutions that make for a more interdependent world. The main actors of the world stage are no longer only national actors, but include *transnational, international* and *supranational* agents. These are both regional and functional, private and public, affecting every sphere of social activity.

The contemporary global system is a mesh of inter-related groups which share an increasingly crowded planet of finite and exhaustible resources. Under the circumstances, world politics is a process by which these disparate groups try to adapt to each other, set and attain goals, as well as resolve issues common to their separate and competing jurisdictions in the shrinking environment within which they must coexist.

The increasing movement of goods, services, people, messages, capital and energy has produced a dynamic international system of highly interacting and interrelated parts. What happens in one region affects the others, and it seems that the complexity of these relationships will soon make everything depend on everything else.

In these conditions there is no question of any territorial or functional group being able to act independently in any significant matter. Important private and public policies must be negotiated, coordinated, compromised, and adapted to fit into each other. Not doing so creates frictions, confrontations, conflicts and violence. The necessity for policy complementarity and international cooperation becomes crucial for the survival of the system.

As the world becomes more complex, interconnected, and highly technological, it also becomes more delicate and fragile. The slightest malfunction in one place can be magnified with disastrous effects in another. A minor disruption in one part can wreak havoc in another distant and indirectly related part. This increasing vulnerability of the modern industrial system makes even an apparently insignificant accident or sabotage extremely dangerous to the stability of the world, because of the non-linear cause-effect chains of chaotic systems. The delicate equilibrium of complex mechanisms is easily prone to large-scale breakdowns; so organized life in the "global village" becomes a difficult and exacting process.

Since only an isolated state can be truly independent and only a subsistence economy can be self-sufficient, contemporary societies depend on the increased application of international laws to regulate their relations. The so-called "free-market" or "state-sovereignty" are anachronistic slogans which bear no relation to the realities of the global techno-economic complex.

Ecosystem Entropy

From what we have said so far it seems that the most crucial problems of the world are global in scope; for that reason the locus of significant decision-making is shifting to the international scene. Although it is now evident that public policies, whether regional or global, can only be successful by the cooperation of those concerned, the leaders of the world have not yet found an acceptable formula to legitimize such cooperation. There is an apparent weariness and a widespread search for new directions, since many people believe that mankind is at a turning point of its history.

Yet, even though the long-term interests of mankind are identical, the short-term interests of different countries diverge. The countless differences of culture and power of nations create different perceptions and interpretations of their interests and values. Where they all agree is the desirability of material wealth. Accordingly, states encourage the consumption of materials they do not have; regions attract masses of people they cannot sustain; and corporations create demands for goods they cannot supply. The basic behavioral pattern of the world system is exponential growth of all its indicators, something that cannot end up in anything but collapse. If these trends continue, the limits to growth will be reached within the next century due to the positive feedback loops that they generate.

Trying to raise the entire world to present western standards would require a tenfold increase of the present Gross World Product; a growth that even if possible would be catastrophic for the ecosystem. It seems that the environment can support either a few rich and many poor or many moderately well-off, but it cannot make everybody rich without collapsing from its own weight. Anyone advocating both closing the rich-poor gap and at the same time increasing economic growth across the board is proposing two irreconcilable policies.

The forecasts of recent trends and their sociopolitical consequences add up to a most dismal and nightmarish vision of the future. It is a specter of degradation and indignity, disorder and injustice, misery and fatalism for the majority of mankind. This movement towards a behavioral sink is being brought about by unhealthy conditions resulting in pathological conduct and extremism. Environmental pressures can be expected to accentuate these trends leading to many militaristic, totalitarian, imperialistic, and nihilistic movements. These dangerous proclivities tend to be self-enforcing, lock-in situations, where systemic pressures set up forces which perpetuate patterns of inertia and entropy, thus placing the system beyond the control of human intervention.

Geopolitical Conflicts

So far, we looked upon the world as a single system and outlined its macrosocial trends. Now, we must delve more closely into the major subsystems which are involved in the most critical geopolitical conflicts of this century. This section focuses on the greatest dichotomies of the twentieth century: East West and North South. The confrontations in these two cross-cutting camps dominate the recent past, present and foreseeable future of world politics. As a result, the two crucial issues of economic development and international coalitions will determine to a great extent what happens to any country in the coming decades.

East West Geopolitics

The outer limits of the framework upon which the world system operated for almost half century after the Second World War were set by the relations between East and West, dominated by the United States and the Soviet Union, whose nuclear potential set the margins of action in all international relations. Mutual and balanced nuclear deterrence was an umbrella under which conventional and limited violence was permissible in the peripheries while peaceful coexistence could be the only condition at the center of the system.

Beyond coexistence, however, the evolving detente between the two power centers reflected the converging interests of all industrial economies in the face of new external pressures. So much so that this evolution took a revolutionary turn circa 1990 when the traditional East West divide was completely effaced. Within a very short time, the arms race was reversed, the Eastern Block was dismantled and the Soviet Union disappeared from the face of the earth. As a result, the West emerged as the nominal victor with the USA as its only super-power.

Yet, the former East West militaro-ideological confrontation was replaced by another East West politico-cultural contradiction. The disintegration of Soviet power and communist doctrine coincided with the rise of nationalist fervor and fundamentalist movements. The repressive totalitarian bloc of Eastern Europe was replaced by its fractured nationalist regimes and oppressive reactionary religions of Middle Eastern Afro-Asia. As a natural reaction to rampant capitalism, liberalism and transnationalism, oriental tribalism and fundamentalism has now become the major antagonist of occidental modernism and cosmopolitanism.

From the point of view of *ecosocialism*, both Eastern and Western ideals have major drawbacks. Although ecologically benign, the former is sociologically unacceptable. Similarly, although the latter is ecologically malignant, it is historically unavoidable. It is, thus, inconceivable that the fundamentalist solution can realistically be applied to the problems of industrialism for most of the world. It is our thesis here that the third road of ecosocialism seems to offer the optimal potential, if not for a definitive solution, at least for a sustainable amelioration of the global problematic.

North South Socioeconomics

Overlapping the cultural schism between the Occident and the Orient, there looms the economic chasm between the Northern and Southern hemispheres. Moreover, both these ideological and material gaps are increasing in absolute and relative terms. The world is rapidly torn apart by the deepening division between its urban affluent centers in the northern continents and its rural poverty stricken regions in the southern.

Because of their economic differences, the problems of the two worlds are different. Whereas resource depletion and environmental degradation are heading the issues of the wealthy countries; poverty, famine, and weakness are the top issues of the underdeveloped ones. Any suggestion of an ecosociety in the Third World, therefore, seems misplaced, if not positively indecent.

The different problems of the North and South correspond to their opposing interests which create continuous conflicts. These conflicts arise from the different range of policies and relationships to material resources. The wealthy societies are increasingly lengthening their range of planning to longer and wider issues, whereas the poorer countries are primarily concerned with the immediate and local problems engulfing them. Short-term advantages for one side mean long-term disadvantages for the other and vice versa. As suppliers of raw materials, the underdeveloped nations are in direct confrontation with the insatiable users of these goods, that is, the overdeveloped systems.

The increasing interdependence of the two sides makes them mutually vulnerable to unilateral moves. As the poor countries depend upon the rich for capital and technology, the rich depend on the poor for raw materials and energy. The technology which allows the wealthy societies to consume so much, also makes them highly exposed to any disruption of their input. Because they have more to lose, the *haves* are more prone to blackmail from the *have-nots*. Retaliatory policies and counter-attacks, if they lock into escalation spirals, would exacerbate the problems of both sides and bring closer the day of reckoning which threatens the whole system.

Unfortunately, the only power the poor have is their potential for disruption; so if the rich do not leave them any alternative, it would be unrealistic to expect them not to use their ultimate weapon. Unless the trends which widen the economic gap are reversed, desperate behavior might also increase and along with it the counter-measures of terror will paralyze any orderly development of the world.

Industrial Development Confrontation

The stratified international system, with its discrepancies in wealth, power, and prestige has created a structure of dependence and inferiority in the nations of the Third World. The elites of these countries feel a sense of *atimia* which they want to overcome by intense emulation of the northern model of technological advance and industrial development. Once the process of power accumulation gets under way it tends to feed upon itself, making it more difficult for others to catch up. For those left out, the impression that not only are they useless, but hopeless, creates a feeling of futility and frustration. From this condition, there is only a small step to resentment and violence against those allegedly responsible or against any scapegoat readily available for that matter.

Moreover, economic development is becoming increasingly costly. The wasteful practices of the initial industrializers cannot be duplicated on a larger scale because of the depletion of resources and the increasing cost of their exploitation. The days of almost free raw materials, which have been partly responsible for the high standard of living of the industrial nations, are over. Whereas previously the rich could urge the poor to wait for the benefits of growth to trickle down to them eventually, the limits to growth now make such waiting an incredible farce.

Lacking both food and capital, the economies of the poorer countries are caught in a vicious circle from which they cannot escape without heavy external help. The economic prospects for many underdeveloped countries are bleak. For over a billion people, the future only holds deteriorating socioeconomic conditions. The increasing scarcity and expense of energy will wipe out any gains that these countries made in the past, as it slows down, if not ends the growth of the rich.

These projections of economic stagnation and, in many cases, deterioration will make the least developed countries the real losers of the coming decades. Such threat does not leave them with many alternatives. Their leaders could either accept their poverty and dependence upon the philanthropy of the rich countries, furthering the neo-imperialistic tendencies of the latter, or they could fall into radical solutions for a desperate fight against their fate. Assuming that some countries at least will opt for the second alternative, the certainty of increased national and international conflict becomes evident. Unless we find a way out of this dilemma and increase the options of these people, the new century will open in very unpleasant atmosphere.

Emerging Interest Coalitions

As described so far, the international system is characterized by an uneven distribution of power and wealth. Ethnic, geographic, functional and other forms of power concentration coexist and conflict with each other. National groups, sovereign states, transnational corporations, international movements, supranational communities, all compete for the loyalties of people. The ideological and military blocs of the middle of the century are giving way to new alignments based on shifting cultural and financial interests.

Economic cartels and resource syndicates are trying to offset traditional military and political powers. In spite of their heterogeneity, Third World people are trying to coordinate their activities for mutual help. South South relations are therefore increasing and regional cooperation is institutionalized. As a result, the South cannot be considered as a monolithic bloc.

On the contrary, it is fragmenting into several regions of different traits. One is composed of regions rich in resources but poor in industry who aim to cash-in their depletable raw materials to the highest bidder before they run out of them. Another has the opposite profile of postindustialization in spite of no natural resources, and is fast approaching the cutting edge of technological progress. On the other extreme is a third category of those who have neither and are sinking deeper into the black hole of despair and destruction. In between is most of the Southern world who is at the crossroads of its development and might go either way: up or downhill.

Facing all these people are the Northern commodity producers and resource consumers are trying to maintain their privilege and consolidate their power. Yet, no matter how efficient and conserver the postindustrial economies become, they cannot escape their interdependence with importing matters and exporting markets. Their only choice is the degree and timing of such interdependence. Ultimately, the industrial nations will have to decide what price they want to pay in both social and economic terms for this condition. The decisions made by all concerned in this century will have lasting effects for a long time to come, because they will set up the new rules of the game for the international system.

Meanwhile, in this period of rapid transition, where the old rules are no longer viable and new rules have not yet become legitimized -misunderstandings and conflicts are the order of the day. The rising central issues relating to the production, distribution and consumption of matter or energy are tearing the world apart. Moreover, the dualistic structures of the international system promote these divisions and gaps into frictions and confrontations, so much so that conflict is a major consumer of social energies.

In periods of uncertainty, such as the present, groups and individuals attach inordinate importance to the possession of concrete goods and raw materials, because they can be easily converted to energy which is the ultimate measure of life. The natural abhorrence that every organism has for death leads to this struggle for self-preservation which can escalate into systemic self-destruction. For this reason, control of natural resources and means of production is such an important factor of world politics.

Nation-State Sovereignty

As we proceed from the macropolitical parameters of the world system, through mesopolitical relationships of regional and functional sub-systems, to the micropolitical interactions within nations, we now come to investigate the intranational factors which significantly affect the overall system. These factors can be easily grouped around the most dominant ideology of our times: nationalism. It is this great force that characterizes the structure of world politics and provides the majority of international actors with their principal roles. Therefore, any attempt to reconstitute society along more ecological lines cannot leave nationalism out of the picture.

National Independence

In spite, or because of increasing technoeconomic interdependence, the world is experiencing an opposite increase of ethnopolitic independence. The global system seems to be undergoing two simultaneous and contradictory trends: a centripetal one that ties its components closer to each other, and a centrifugal one that renders them asunder. These contradictory movements increase the stresses and strains of an already fragile system and add to its chances of breakdown.

The paradox is that as the infrastructure of the world becomes more inextricably interwoven, the suprastructure is moving in the opposite direction of greater self-determination. While societies converge their cultures by the spreading process of modernization and industrialization, people demand increased autonomy to decide their own matters and make their own policies locally, at the same time as they raise a louder voice in world affairs.

As a result of these divisive and contradictory forces, the political system of the world becomes much more decentralized. The breakdown of empires and blocs followed the world-wide movement of decolonization and nation-building in the new states of Africa and Asia. Great power dominance becomes increasingly unacceptable to most of the smaller states, whose collective pressures multiply the effect of their demands.

The diffusion of power into a multipolar structure means that no state is strong enough to impose its will or even benevolence over the whole system. The balance of power is maintained by a large number of governing elites in key states who seek to maximize their interests at the expense of each other. The trouble is that this balance is inherently unstable because the internally independent dynamics of each state produce hostile self-aggravating deadlocks which threaten the whole system.

States as International Actors

Never has the world undergone such a large scale change in such a short time as in the twentieth century. Yet, states still remain the main actors in the world arena, because they are supposed to control social disorders and oppose foreign threats. This supreme *raison d'état* has justified their monopoly of legitimate violence and ensures their place in the sun.

Although from the point of view of every state, military defence seems to be the only "rational" response to external threat, from the point of view of the world the aggregate effects of all these actions operate as a self-fulfilling prophesy. The mere existence of such multiplicity of power centers creates a sense of insecurity amongst them which they try to assuage by strengthening their armaments. Escalation of arms races, nevertheless, have the opposite effect and instead of providing security, they destabilize the system. Power politics becomes a vicious circle, because the omnipresent threat of war justifies the need for states and, at the same time, the existence of states creates the threat of war.

Moreover, increasingly complex issues, interacting events, sophisticated weaponry, and shifting policies, require complicated strategies and innovative thinking which is sadly lacking in the state mentality. National governments are controlled by "entrapped elites" whose attachment to the mythology of nationalism and etatism leaves them no choice but to continue the same narrow policies which perpetuate their discontent. It is evident by now that states can hardly protect their societies from megaproblems which they neither understand nor control.

This protection is not only strictly military defence, but ecosystem survival in the broad sense which totally escapes the purview of independent state action. The rapidly developing environmental and resource crises in the world scale cannot be resolved by the principles of sovereignty, and so states are caught in an impasse of impotence and fatalism. What is worse, trying to solve these problems unilaterally within a state's own jurisdiction, exacerbates the very same problems outside its borders, thus increasing the dangers of backlash.

States, of course, are forced to compromise their sovereignty by trading parts of it when there is no other way out; but such trade-offs are half-way measures that solve one problem only to create another. As long as the basic structures of power-politics and state-rationale persist, global problems will only be temporarily and partially solved. The inescapable conclusion is that national governments alone cannot resolve global issues, because the most lethal threats to the world are due to the fact that legally independent states are trapped in an exponentially shrinking space and time.

States as Intranational Actors

The ostensible reason of external security is not the only function of the state. Internal peace and order is the other side of the sovereignty coin. To its passive role of policeman, the state has added many more active roles of social control and intervention. Most people now take it for granted that the state is responsible for social progress in general and economic development in particular. Governments come under increased pressure to become more involved in all aspects of social life and are thereby held responsible if anything goes wrong.

Rapid technological and radical social changes, however, are often too much for any government to cope with, so many of them are swept aside by more authoritarian leaders. Under such critical periods of rising expectations and declining resources, strong regimes can either try to pull society out of its downward spiral or freeze the *status quo* expecting to stem any further change.

Social demands, moreover, are not usually complementary to each other. Different interests in society push or pull governments in opposite directions. The segments of the population which demand change clash with the vested interests which oppose it. These contradictory pressures place an onerous burden upon political leadership and the resulting conflicts are enough to try any system.

All regimes, irrespective of their ideology, have to promote the interests of those groups upon which they depend for their support. In abnormal situations, either the controlling groups are the privileged segments of society which try to suppress popular dissatisfaction by force, or they are revolutionary movements aiming to mobilize social energies for radical change. In either case, force is unavoidably manifested in domestic violence or foreign aggression. As a result, continuing political instability in many regions of the world, brought about by weak unresponsive rulers, as well as international conflicts precipitated by strong radical movements, may be expexted.

Added to these conflicts is the one between rapid economic growth and more equitable social distribution of wealth. This contradiction stems from the fact that it is possible for a country's GNP to be rising, while at the same time the equality between social classes to be falling. Economic development, therefore, not only does not guarantee social stability, but is intrinsically disruptive. A positive correlation has been found between socioeconomic change and geopolitical instability, thus supporting this pessimistic conclusion.

Many modernizing nations are engaged in altering traditional structures and values in a climate of violent confrontation and spreading misery. The growing consciousness of the miserables of this earth inevitably leads them to the conclusion that they have nothing to lose by revolting against their rulers or forcing their governments to war.

Ethnic Movements of Separatism

States not only have to fight against the supranational forces which tend to diminish their sovereignty, but also the subnational forces which try to divide them. The same political units that oppose economic interdependence must, in turn, maintain their internal unity in the face of divisive trends within their borders. The same centrifugal tendencies that destroyed continental empires continue their work in trying to break down present states into smaller and smaller units.

Ethnic groups and regional interests in almost every state make some demands for greater autonomy, if not outright sovereignty. Very few states are homogeneous enough to escape the rising tribalism of their local constituencies. It seems that people everywhere attach themselves to increasingly smaller groups in their demands for self-determination or at least local government. States are, therefore, besieged both from above and from below and have to wage a war on two fronts: internal and external.

Apparently, most of the present states are at once too small and too large. They are too small to carry out their responsibilities and respond to the eventualities that arise and, at the same time, they are too large to create a sense of community among all their people. Global problems are too big even for the superpowers to solve unilaterally; yet local problems also go unsolved even in smaller states.

Statesmen, beleaguered from all sides by mounting problems, turn now to one, then to another, in a haphazard and reactive manner. Some look inwards in a vain effort to satisfy domestic demands and thus neglect pressing problems of international scope.

Others try to escape from the unpleasant truths of their domestic conditions by inventing foreign scapegoats to blame for their troubles. Either way, the problems are not solved but only postponed or transferred to another time or place.

In an increasingly interdependent, more polluted and highly depleted world, state policies of "buying time" or "passing the buck" are both ephemeral and parochial. Ethnocentric behavior may succeed for a while in increasing the benefits of a limited group, but it can only do so at the expense of other nations or future generations.

Mutually exclusive and conflicting national policies promote these unequal and self-contradictory developments and then try to resolve them in isolation. Without integral planning and systemic action, world scarcity and inequality, as well as degradation and contamination will grow in an accelerating pace. On this bleak note we end this section by emphasizing the looming dangers that the present state system imposes upon the world.

Alternatives

Foreign-Policy Options

The above interpretation of the world situation leaves a country with very few choices. The parameters of the international environment obviously limit a nation's freedom of choice, not only in its foreign, but also in its domestic policy, especially regarding the ecology. In that respect, a state's options could be grouped into three concentric foci: nationalist, continentalist, internationalist. Let us consider the pros and cons of each option, particularly as it concerns ecosociety goals.

Ethnocentric Nationalism

The first type of policy-options can be grouped under the nationalist banner. These options differ in degree between the extremes of "total isolationism," on the one hand, and merely a "our country first" policy, on the other. Within this range of more or less nationalistic policies, a state could choose some feasible compromise which optimizes its national interest. Some nationalist foreign policies which would be compatible with the ideals of an ecosociety are given below.

Independent Foreign Policy

Foreign policy is the net result of a state's perception and pursuit of national interests in the international arena. As such, it is the extension of domestic policies abroad. The growing interdependence of the world makes further distinctions between internal and external affairs rather academic, because any significant activity in one area has a direct impact on the other.

Extending ecosocial ideals to foreign policy is not easy. It is now clear that the amount and manner in which a society uses energy indicates the values it espouses and has far reaching consequences both on its internal institutions and external relations. For that reason, any fundamental change in this respect is a profoundly unsettling experience.

The crucial question is whether a particular state is able to effect such dramatic social change, given its geopolitical situation in the world. Obviously, great powers have a better chance of getting their way in the world than smaller states, who have to make up their lesser material power with better political prowess. Their foreign policy has to be as flexible and innovative as possible, probing the limits of their capacity to bring about desired changes.

The National Interest

A foreign policy is nationalistic to the extent that it promotes the national interest and external independence of the country. Since a state's paramount national interest may be defined as "internal unity and external independence," a nationalist foreign policy aims to reduce the country's dependence on any foreign state, at the same time as it builds up the nation's collective identity.

In order to attain this aim, one cannot underestimate the relation between national interest and nationalist sentiment. In any case, a modicum of nationalism is necessary to provide a country with the will to survive as single state. Without such unifying sentiment, the centrifugal forces within a country and external forces beyond it are there to do the job. Only a strong national vision and leadership can hope to counter the divisive trends which are in evidence everywhere.

Although an extremely nationalistic interpretation of the national interest is both dangerous and counterproductive, a healthy patriotic sentiment is both necessary and desirable. In the name of sovereignty, nationalism protects ethnic groups from internal dissolution and external penetration. By doing so, it opposes the imperialism or colonialism by which powerful countries exploit smaller ones.

For a country to minimize its foreign dependence and resist the siren song of consumerism, it must develop a strong national consciousness. The extraordinary effort required to effect such social change needs the generating force of a collective single-mindedness which only nationalism can provide. An optimal foreign policy, therefore, assumes that the national interest has a pragmatic priority over everything else.

The common interest may be seen as a collective consumption good. As the protector and promoter of such interest, nationalism fulfills many functions. Its benefits accrue to both individuals and groups because a great deal of psychological satisfaction is derived from nationalist sentiments. For that reason, material advantages or deprivations become secondary; so that a nation might be willing to sacrifice some of its physical comforts, in order to gain more in national spirit.

If that is socially acceptable, the economic costs necessary for the move towards an ecosociety could be willingly born by a community having a well-developed sense of national identity. In this case, ecosocial goals can become the core values around which people can rally to effect their nation-building.

From Independence to Isolationism

In the contemporary world, national identity and political independence are relative terms. As was already mentioned, modern economic interdependence and cultural convergence makes either absolute autarchy or autarky rather unrealistic. No country can live in isolation for any length of time, without making extraordinary sacrifices and paying a heavy price. Nations, like individuals, learn to live together and be come more or less socialized.

A modest nationalism then steers between the extremes of aggressive interventionism in the affairs of other states and isolationist withdrawal from the international system. Privileged states cannot expect to be left alone to enjoy their splendid isolation, while the rest of the world is going down the drain. Trying to create an ecosociety in one coutry by ignoring what is going on outside its borders would be like building an oasis in the middle of the desert. Unfortunately, this is no longer feasible, since there are no isolated spots left in the world.

Retreating into one's shell is a reflex defensive action of many species when faced with a hostile environment. Likewise, rich societies or groups may be tempted to entrench themselves and hoard their resources in the face of external encroachments. Yet, whether by human sentiment or philanthropic tradition, it is unlikely that such ethnocentric egoism could prevail.

If each state responds only to immediate internal pressures and does not cooperate with others in resolving long-range global issues, the international system will surely break down and its units will revert to protectionism, parochialism and isolationism. Such disintegration will strengthen the ghettos of affluence and privilege struggling to resist the mounting tide of poverty and despair of the world's masses. In that case, the social collapse accompanying this conflict is much more imminent than the physical limits of the natural system.

Although there are certain disquieting indications that the foreign policies of some postindistrial countries may be hardening as external pressures are rising and demands for sharing the world's wealth multiply, it should be understood that any "us-against-them" strategies pay only in the short run, while they become disastrous in the long one. So, by past tradition, present interest, and future goals, most countries could not be divorced from the world, even if they wanted.

Not only would isolationism be impossible for trading and consuming nations, it would be almost out of the question for a modern state to become an ecosociety in isolation. Some understanding and cooperation from one's partners or neighbors would be indispensable, if one is to bring about such change. So, as the task of domestic policy is to prepare people for the transition to the ecosociety, the task of foreign policy is to make this transformation as agreeable as possible to other concerned states.

Economic Nationalism

If national independence is neither isolationism nor unilateralism, the question becomes what kind of independence, where, from whom and at what cost? If dependence in a single foreign country is incompatible with nationalism, how can one avoid it?

Any independent policy-making would be a chimera without control of one's technological and industrial institutions. Only when the economic system becomes responsive to the needs and wishes of its own people, is a country able to develop a national culture and identity. One does not have to be xenophobic to realize that foreign ownership in most cases exploits human labor and natural resources for immediate profit, without bothering with sustainable development. A high degree of foreign control usually leads to an undue emphasis on economic growth and imposes strict limits to one's ability to create an ecosociety. Thus, any movement in this direction must go on in parallel with greater control of one's economy.

A conserver society must be able to live much more within its means than a consumer society. In the present, the accelerating pace of international trade is tied to the continuing growth of the consumer economy. This process can only go on until shortage of the traded goods or refusal to to pay their price is encountered. At that time, hoarding can be expected to contract the commercial activities and the standard of living of those countries which have overextended themselves. If a country is not to be drawn in this escalating spiral, trade should be restricted within the conserver framework of economic nationalism.

Although absolute self-sufficiency, like isolationism, is neither possible nor desirable in the contemporary world; a moderate economic nationalism promotes a healthy self-reliance which optimizes self-sufficiency. Thus, for a country wealthy in natural and human resources, it would be quite possible to improve its autonomy along with the conservation of its resources.

A respectable economic nationalism is indispensable, not only to political but also to ecological independence. That means that an ecosociety must impose stringent controls in the exploitation and degradation of primary non-renewable natural resources, in order to insulate its ecosystem as much as possible from external destructive influences. Such protectionist policy may be supported by a majority, as long as more equitable distribution of the national wealth is also effected.

Regional Supranationalism

National independence does not mean that a country is uncooperative in promoting its complementary interests with others. A pragmatic foreign policy decides each case on its own merits and does not simply follow any dogma or other state. That is, given the national interest, as it is perceived and determined by its people, a government may enter into various associations with other states for purposes of mutual benefit.

The question is what kind of associations, and with whom, will be compatible with an ecosociety. The minimal option is carrying out some neighborly conduct of mutual benefit and the maximal is joining some supranational system for the common good. Since the first option has already been covered, this section will concentrate on the possibility and desirability of a supranational ecosociety.

Supranational Integration

The trend towards greater international interdependence is presently moving into its next phase out of which emerges supranational integration. Many areas of the world have attempted to institutionalize their economic interdependence by forming common markets, custom unions, or free-trade areas. Among them, the First World is the most successful in this direction because it is the most integrated in its overall development.

The only actual case of supranationalism is to be found in Western Europe. Presently, however, North America is moving in the same direction and might reach supranational status early in the next century. Beyond these ongoing cases, a third probability is the institutionalization of Pacific Oceania in the next century. When this happens, the postmodern world will be composed of three centers of power (Germany, U.S.A., Japan) and their respective spheres of influence (Europa, America, Oceania).

This supranational movement consolidates power into three supergroups which dominate world politics and economics, as well as trade and finance. Unfortunately, the proliferation of exclusive economic blocs not only perpetuates the present intercontinental inequalities but further exacerbate them. Those left outside find themselves in a distinct commercial disadvantage and so gravitate towards the closest of these economic blocs.

Nevertheless, an ecosociety would be in a better position to withstand foreign trade pressures, because it would be less vulnerable to external economic forces. Moreover, an ecosociety could hardly exist as part of a consumer common market. Either the entire system adopts conserver policies or none of its members could. For that reason, one has to choose very carefully one's economic partners for their ecopolitical compatibilities

The European Union

The European Union (E.U.) is a supranational system of twelve states in Western Europe, which within barely fifty years since its inception is slated to become the first peaceful confederation of the old continent. As this is happening, the three European great powers (England, Germany, France), together with their nine smaller partners, are uniting to form an economic and political union of superpower proportions. So much so, that Europe is in the process of recapturing its traditional role as the center of the world affairs once again.

The powerful attraction of the E.U. is bringing the other Western European states to its door, so that it is expected that before the end of the century, the seven EFTA (European Free Trade Area) countries will become its members. Beyond that, the recently liberated Eastern European countries will eventually join to complete the continental confederation within the next generation.

Meanwhile, the question is whether this evolution augurs well for the development of a continental ecosociety. Although it is too early to tell yet, various sociopolitical trends point in that direction. Environmental consciousness is quite high in the E.U. and its ecopolicies reflect this fact. It should not be forgotten that the ecopolitical movement began in Europe and the popularity of Green parties is highest there.

With these precedents, it seems that the E.U. could become the first postmodern ecosociety in the world; so joining it would not be detrimental to the environmental movement of any society. Although being part of a supranational system necessarily means some surrender of national sovereignty, the trade offs from such exchange might make it worthwhile.

Given the prevailing conditions, a European country can hardly resist the attraction of the E.U. A country's geopolitical and socio-economic position determines the parameters of freedom of action and places great constraints upon independence. This does not mean that there is no room for some maneuvering within these parameters so as to maximize one's range of options. A lot can be done to keep control over a country's economy and culture as it joins a supranational jurisdiction.

American Continentalism

Following the successful example of the EU, other continental attempts are being made to create free trade areas as the first step to a common market. The most advanced of these is presently going on in North America, where the unique geopolitical relationship which the United States has with Canada and Mexico makes economic integration a distinct possibility.

U.S.A. and Canada (the world's first and tenth largest economies), have the highest bilateral trade and investment links in the world, even though they are not officially a common market. Although Canada and Mexico derive certain economic benefits from their ties with the U.S., they also suffer definite political disadvantages. As long as economic growth is a top priority, such socio-political sacrifices can be justified. However, if one of the smaller parties moves towards an ecosociety, such high degree of interdependence is not only unnecessary but positively harmful, unless the dominant partner also adopts an ecosocial philosophy.

An independent national stand need not be anti-American. On the contrary, it should try to export the ecosociety ideals to the U.S. The great differences in power between the U.S. and its neighbors make any continental relationship necessarily unequal. Partnerships in which one side is ten times as powerful as the other will necessarily be lopsided. Even if the smaller partners do not suffer exploitation but, on the contrary, receive special benefits, such unequal relation does not help their psychological maturity and self-respect. Any asymmetrical relationship, even if it is benevolent paternalism, means the domination of the smaller partner by the larger.

The Americanization of the World is, of course, a cliché by now. All Western economic structures, not to speak of entire social cultures, largely reflect American ideals. Moreover, the gap between one's technological and capital resources cannot but perpetuate the dependence on the U.S. If the interdependence between countries continues, it would become impossible to reverse, and the result would inevitably be the economic, cultural and ultimately political absorption of both Mexico and Canada into the North American giant.

A large segment of public opinion seems to demand a reversal of continental integrationism. Even if a lower standard of living will result, many people are prepared to accept it in order to promote their national independence. In order to counter a superpower's gravitational pull, smaller states have to strengthen their internal solidarity and external relations; so that they do not have to look to any single source for their economic survival.

If that is not possible, then a concerted effort must be made to move the entire continental system towards an ecosociety. Such a daunting task is a long-range project that requires international cooperation on a large scale. Converting the bastion of consumerism into conservationism could then be the ultimate challenge of any global ecopolicy.

The First and the Third World

It is important that regional associations of the First World not be interpreted by the Third World as a collusion of the rich to despoil or even abandon the poor. Powerful blocs, whether ideological or economic, tend to polarize the world and, hence, increase the magnitude of its confrontations. As long as there is a multitude of independent centers of power, dichotomies are attenuated and their conflicts diffused.

Moreover, national interests do not always fit standard categories. Although a country may be rich and industrialized, it may also be a raw material producer and energy exporter. As such, its interests overlap both First and Third Worlds. Some kind of association with energy producers and commodity exporters would not only be advantageous but help to stabilize the balance of power in the world.

A postindustrial country's association in many international organizations exchanges influence among them, thus combating exclusiveness and making them more outward-looking. Bridging the gap between these different worlds could be the most worthy of a country's external objectives.

In order to enhance a country's credibility with the Third World, one must be dissociated from any neo-imperialist adventures. On the contrary, helping the Third World not only has moral but economic and political advantages. The Third World, the most populous and critical area of the planet, presents the worst dangers as well as the best opportunities for mankind.

As the developments in the United Nations indicate, the Third World's power and potential cannot be ignored any longer. It would be both realistic and moral for a country to strengthen its ties with the masses of the world. Such ties would be particularly apt for an ecosociety, because it can show them a different road to development and independence. As a first step in this direction, Northern states should help energy and raw material producers to improve their terms of trade.

Global Internationalism

As our foreign policy horizons widen, we move from a merely ethnocentric viewpoint, through a broader regional perspective, to the all-inclusive world-view. Foreign policy must try to bring together these three spheres of interest to the point of making them complimentary. For this reason, we now put forth the global requirements of foreign policy within which the regional and national interests are also included. In the contemporary world, only a global perspective can serve as the criterion for an enlightened foreign policy for any nation.

Inclusive Multilateralism

A postindustrial society is usually of multicultural composition with some experience on how to deal in a heterogeneous world. The people of such society should feel at home in a world of different traditions and be able to adjust more easily to variations in life styles. Indeed, a multicultural identity could be built upon the broad principles of an "international nationalism" which combines elements of many cultures without fusing them altogether.

Moreover, a federal structure and decentralized institutions resemble in many respects the international system, so experience in running intrafederal affairs is very relevant in intergovernmental relations. If the process of developing an international nation could be combined with an ecosociety, such country could become truly a model for the world.

National independence is not necessarily contradictory to international cooperation. On the contrary, greater independence and equality among nations would make cooperation more voluntary and just. The basic principle here is that national problems of any significance can no longer be resolved unilaterally, but require international action. Territorial jurisdiction, therefore, has to be supplemented with functional overlapping authorities. To this end, the concept of state sovereignty is evolving towards a new definition which would fit in with the new realities of the world.

In this process of redefinition, a state can contribute both form and substance. There is no question that enlightened self-interest in the long run can be made to coincide with the common good of mankind. All a state has to make sure is that its short-term interests are not met at the expense of either other nations or the future. Although easier said than done, it is by no means impossible to converge national interests with international benefits: this aim is after all the measure of a moral foreign policy.

Foreign Policy Priorities

A conserver society must change not only the domestic priorities of the consumer society, but also its foreign. An ecological foreign policy will have to go further than platitudinous professions in favor of international peace and justice. Its terms should be defined more precisely in order to dissociate them from the status quo and exploitation. To that end, one should reverse the priorities from: dependence to independence; arming to peacekeeping; bilateralism to multilateralism; and economic growth to balanced development.

To do so, one must work for:

1) recalculation of human priorities from narrow economic to broad social;
2) minimal acceptable standards of consumption and morality;
3) superordinate goals transcending national interests.

Of course, we cannot expect any government to promote policies if they deprive its citizens of their livelihood. Adopting either option alone would be a very unimaginative way of juxtaposing policies. A change that would benefit the world generally would be supported by most people, if all it requires of them is a harmless change of their habits or a minor adjustment in their jobs. To bring this about, a government's duty is to inform and educate its people on the implications that international changes will have on their way of life. Educated people already tend to be rather cosmopolitan, so it would not be difficult for governments to sensitize them to the problems of the world and the responsibility that they have to contribute to their solution.

Since foreign policy is the extension of domestic policy abroad, an ecosociety should try to extend its ideas and experience to other countries. It could become a world leader in ecologically-oriented technology and steady-state economics. A policy of balance between natural supply and human demand which combines resource-conservation with quality of life could become a model for other nations to emulate. By developing special skills in the efficient utilization of resources, especially food production and environmental upgrading, an ecosociety can help other countries with similar problems.

With such help, the world could stop the spread of excessive consumption and pollution patterns and instead substitute new methods of conservation. The most appropriate foreign policy for an ecosociety, therefore, is to transform its ideals into global values and make itself a model for the international community. This endeavor could engage the energies of many people and would be a just basis for their national identity.

Foreign Aid

In a world of misery and injustice, a "Samaritan State" would be a high ideal. Whether or not such ideal can be attained, international aid will still have to be increased. Ecosocieties should make it axiomatic that as members of the rich world, they must share their affluence with the poor.

Distributing 1% of its GNP to those countries that need it more is not an unfair sacrifice for a country to make. This redistribution of wealth, however, can be made in such way as to develop greater self-reliance in the recipients and not perpetuate their dependence. Moreover, the spirit of this distribution must not be that of philanthropy or social welfare but of duty born out of enlightened self-interest.

Obviously, an ecosociety's aid alone will not change much in the world. For this reason, it must operate in conjunction with other similarly inclined countries to ensure a large-scale participation in a cooperative struggle to overcome world poverty and inhumanity. To that end multilateral rather than bilateral action should be emphasized, so that the whole international community, and not merely the donors, decide the parameters of the aid.

Such distribution need not make the recipients a replica of the donors. If the world is to move in the direction of conservation, an ecosociety can help developing countries by:

1) transfering more intermediate or appropriate technology;
2) improving food production for the domestic market;
3) promoting rural development and agricultural reform;
4) creating labor-intensive occupations in light industry.

All these projects, needless to say, must be undertaken with the consultation and cooperation of all those concerned.

Development aid must not necessarily be limited to intergovernmental cooperation. Any regime should not automatically be helped simply because it is in *de facto* control of a disadvantaged country. It is well-known that helping certain governments not only does nothing for their people but strengthens the rulers stronghold over the masses. One must be dissociated from reactionary and wasteful elites, whose affinities and interests tie them to powerful foreign influences rather than their own people.

On the contrary, support should go to progressive elements in those countries who struggle to resolve rather than suppress their problems. Once ecosocial values are decided, one must not be afraid to help those who share these goals, whether they are in power or in opposition. In other words, aid should not only be economic but political, since economic development in itself does not mean political reform, let alone social progress. There is nothing wrong in tying development aid to political considerations, so that external help benefits those who share conservationist ideas and reformist policies in their countries.

Activist Diplomacy

An ecosociety is hardly likely to be maintained in one country alone. An ecopolicy must make its thrust in both the domestic and foreign arenas. To do so in the latter, diplomacy must pull its end by influencing other states to move in the same direction. An ecosociety must make its voice heard in the world more tridently than others. If one has something to contribute in improving the world, it becomes a duty to spread it far and wide. If there is any hope in averting a global catastrophe, it is for prosperous and stable countries to become ecosociety models, so that by their words and deeds they show the world an alternative way of life.

Most people tend to underestimate themselves and their capabilities, particularly in international affairs. The role of smaller countries in the world has been passive and supporting, like good soldiers in the camp of one or another of the great powers. The dramatic economic and political changes in the international system during the last few years, however, have shaken the stronghold of the great powers upon the world. In the new emerging world order, the distribution of power promises to be wider, so more states will take an active international role.

National power cannot be measured solely by productions or battalions. Purely material or brutally destructive power have very limited application and their ability to win friends and influence people is rather circumspect. Pay-offs or threats can go so far before they become counter-productive; whereas national integrity and diplomatic acumen go a longer way in establishing one's international credibility.

Smaller states can then capitalize on their relatively clean past as well as their lack of threatening

power. A middle power can do things which neither
a superpowers not a mini-state can undertake. To do
so, their diplomacy must become bolder and newer,
more daring and activist. Taking up the ecosocial
cause in the world serves to give the proper purpose
to diplomatic activism and thus orient a country's
efforts in the right direction.

The Global System

A World Ecosociety

The point has finally been reached where we must
consider the necessary political changes in the international system, if the world is to become an ecosociety. Assuming the application of enough interdependent and internationalist foreign policies upon a
responsive world, the road towards a global ecosociety will be open. This last section looks into the three
main areas of inevitable change by which the world
could be transformed into an ecosociety.

Earth Politics

For our purposes, the central arena for social change
is that of politics. In general, power-politics is the
process by which the present system is controlled. In
order to change this system of power relations by the
next century, world politics will have to tackle and
resolve the two main global issues presently out-
standing: social (economic, political, and cultural)
development and natural (energetic, material, environmental) containment. In that respect, the following points should be considered.

Possible Trend Scenarios

Among the countless different possibilities open to the world, there are only a few probable alternatives for the turn of this century. In the case of the central issue that concerns us here, change in the direction of an ecosociety will come about by:

1) drift until rising pressures and depleting resources suppress growth;
2) evolutionary stemming of consuming habits and polluting ways of life;
3) planned systematic international movement to reverse the trends;

These three outcomes exhaust our anticipations; assuming that the ecosystem cannot possibly go on indefinitely supporting exponential growth. In the first case, if nothing is done, a conserver society will arise out of the ruins of the consumer society after the deluge. For the pessimists, this is the most likely outcome. The optimists, on the other hand, hope that somehow the people of the world will eventually realize the danger while there is still time and voluntarily renounce their evil ways.

Between the disastrous destruction and the miraculous transformation, a more realistic scenario is that people and their governments could effect the change by combining enlightened self-interest with improved high-technology. Although the optimistic alternative is most desirable and the pessimistic most probable, the third possibility is the best way of balancing the external threat of natural catastrophe with our internal dread of social atrophy.

The Politics of Redistribution

Assuming that a resolution for the major international issues is possible, the crucial political problem of the world becomes the redistribution of its wealth. In that case, sociopolitics tries to find a way of putting a floor under the standard of living of everyone by transfering the surplus income above a certain maximum from those who have surpassed this ceiling to those who have not reached the floor. Establishing an acceptable range of human consumption would not only alleviate human misery of those who do not have enough, but improve the quality of life of those who have too much. Intergroup transfers would both attain a more equitable distribution of wealth and a more ecological equilibrium between human activities and the supporting environment.

To attain the twin conditions of environmental balance and social justice, ecopolitics seeks a global steady-state in which most growth should and could take place in the service sectors, transfer economies, recyclable goods, and qualitative aspects of life.

Obviously, all these areas raise thorny political issues. How could the powerful be persuaded to share their privileges with the wretched of the earth? At the same time, how could the wealthy be asked to limit their absolute growth which has some trickle-down effect, improving somewhat the lot of the poor. Since the international system does not possess the power to tax the rich, how could such redistribution be made?

Given these constraints, the political option is enlightened self-interest on the part of the *haves* combined with sufficient political pressures from the *have-nots*. If they are properly organized, the many can multiply their power and overcome the resistance of the few. This is clearly the "game" of world politics for the foreseeable future.

The world-game need not be zero-sum. A net transfer of resources could be effected in such a way as to maximize the gains of the poor and also minimize the losses of the rich. The difference has to be made up by a change in psychology and efficiency. After reaching a certain level of consumption and education, people shift their attention to non-material pursuits which allow gains in quality of life without losses in standard of living. In this way, the rich can give up significant material privileges without feeling the quantitative loss which in effect is converted into a qualitative gain.

In order to attain both the ecosociety in the wealthy countries and the humane society in the poor ones, ecopolitics must succeed in redistributing resources as well as rechanneling expectations. To that end, people everywhere should cooperate in setting international standards of human welfare and then press for a more equitable distribution of the world's wealth to meet these standards.

Political Development

A shift of emphasis from quantitative material economics to qualitative distributive politics would necessarily require a significant change in individual attitudes and social policies. On the other hand, the collective energy needed to bring about this desired reform is itself generated by the combination of mental changes and material pressures. These interrelated conditions for social change indicate the interdependence among economic, political and cultural development. In order to change the priorities of economic growth, there must be a political catalyst to break social traditions. Alternatively, new ideological innovations and technological inventions act as social enzymes for political development. In any case, a change in one variable produces changes in the others.

Political development is directly proportional to the ability and willingness of a society to absorb or handle change by making its own decisions. This process occurs consciously by collective and deliberate decision-making and conflict-resolving. Finally, policy must be determined after planning alternative futures and weighing different options by the polity as a whole. According to these criteria, all states in a world are somewhat politically underdeveloped. Social changes are usually out of political control, and government reaction to them is haphazard and ineffective.

In this matter, there is very little relationship between economic and political development. In either case, it is not so much material abundance as educational enlightenment and organizational discipline that measure development. As far as that goes, the rich do not seem to show any superior wisdom or greater maturity than the poor. If anything, carrying material accumulation beyond a certain point indicates a singular lack of foresight and perspective.

Integral development involves a structural transformation of the economic and political systems so as to free the potential energy of society for self-perpetuating realization. To do that, society must move towards self-reliance, thus, minimizing its inputs of external energy and giving people a chance to create for themselves the conditions in which they can work towards their self-fulfillment.

In this sense, political development is tied to national self-determination, and comes about when self-control is maximized and power over others is minimized. Humanizing politics in such way requires consciousness-raising and social organization in a large scale. A mature body-politic in world terms is a condition for an international ecosociety, because only by widespread self-control will the system be able to limit its needs.

Conflict and Cooperation

The opposing forces of contradiction and cooperation are in the heart of politics, especially as they are reflected in the international arena. The increasing complexity and interconnectivity of the world system, however, demands a changed mix of these two ingredients. In a fragile and vulnerable system, conflict becomes more dangerous and harmony more imperative. An optimal strategy to avoid collision between culture and nature, as well as confrontation among nations, requires levels of cooperation higher than those we have been used to so far. The necessity born of natural scarcity and a shift of political forces in the world might do the required trick that will bring states together in amicable relations.

Even now, no country can realize its desires without some cooperation from others, and such cooperation is not forthcoming if they too cannot gain something in return. Cooperation becomes the only positive-sum game in the world; whereas, conflict remains at best a zero-sum and, at worst, a negative-sum game. Only by the politics of cooperation can the world solve the techno-economic problems that beset us. It is the main task of ecopolitics to create a sense of common cause among the competing nations by establishing agreed superordinate goals. Once states realize that there are problems that transcend their jurisdictions and can only be solved by a united effort, then they could establish the new rules of the game to attain these goals.

Although cooperation may be imposed by the nature of things, it must nevertheless be accepted and voluntarily implemented by people, because it can only be effective and lasting if it is mutually agreed upon as a collectively beneficial process. The more difficult the problems and the greater the sacrifices, the more people must feel committed to the system in order to apply themselves willingly to the task.

Ecopolitics can create the necessary self-discipline to limit demands and restrain the current obsession with more of everything. The change of direction that is needed in human affairs can best come about by a concerted global strategy worked out by international consensus. Then world politics can move away from power conflicts towards social cooperation. If we are successful in this movement, international politics could become the social biology of collective health for the human race.

World Organization

Perhaps the most important procedural function of international politics is to order the world in such a way as to facilitate the attainment of universal goals and values. Reorganizing the world means providing it with new structures whose function is to promote the ecosociety in a global scale. We now indicate certain trends which point in that direction and propose specific policies to help them along.

Functional Internationalization

The development of international organization is a function of the rate of technological innovation in the world. The birth of international institutions followed the industrial revolution and has been accelerating along with technological change ever since. For more than a century the world has been increasingly regulated in specific technical areas as a result of the increased international interactions.

In the foreseeable future these trends will continue spreading international regulation to the new problem areas of natural resource allocation, pollution control, terms of trade and investment determination, as well as other more particular tasks. One can expect a significant increase in both the breadth and depth of functional interactions in the world.

Accompanying this quantitative increase of functional organization, there is a qualitative development of political internationalization. As the locus of decision-making in functional areas moves from the national to the international arena, there is a spill-over effect into the political areas of policy-making. States find that they have to accept important constraints in their sovereignty, as international institutions take over greater areas of responsibility in legislating, administering and adjudicating new rules of inter-state conduct. Whether national governments like it or not, systemic imperatives are bound to shift political power from the national level to the international.

States do not relish giving up their sovereignty, especially to international institutions where their influence is diluted. But forces beyond their control impose the surrender of significant prerogatives to collective decision-making bodies. As mentioned in the last section, the necessity for international cooperation requires the institutionalization of the political process at the global level. States will have to spend more of their time and effort in intergovernmental organizations, because this is where more and more of the decisions affecting them are made.

Institutional Organization

In spite of the heavy trends, international machinery is not yet adequate to meet the challenges and responsibilities demanded of it. National attitudes are reluctant to provide the necessary means for international institutions to do a good job in creating and enforcing the new rules. Improving this machinery would require both horizontal and vertical reorganization of the international structure.

On the horizontal plane, new regional organizations must supplement the existing ones. The demands of the Third World for a new economic order requires reallocation of power resources among the various regions of the world. To effect these changes the "underdeveloped" countries will be further organizing themselves. In addition, small nations in general find that organization multiplies their power and thus improves their chances to attain their objectives.

Superimposed upon this geographical reorganization, there is a large network of functional organizations, coordinated by the United Nations. Furthermore, Non-Governmental Organizations (NGOs) of various kinds supplement the work of the official agencies. This plethora of international structures has now become too unwieldy and often works at cross purposes. Non-territorial agencies of public and private character will therefore have to be rationalized within a central coordinating body, such as the Economic and Social Council.

Most important, Trans-National Corporations (TNCs) must eventually be incorporated and licensed by the United Nations. Only such a move will put them under the control of the international community and resolve the conflicts that they create as representatives of national extraterritorial jurisdiction. Internationalization provides all the members of the world system with some influence over the policies of these powerful bodies.

For the same reason, internationalization of the high seas and the ocean floor, as well as Antarctica, outer space and celestial bodies, is the only way to ensure the promotion of the common heritage of mankind and place them beyond the particular claims of powerful local groups.

A vertical reorganization of the world reflects the shift of power from the national level, so states can disengage from many functions which can better be performed either at higher or lower levels. Strengthening the infra- and supra-national level will bring about a more balanced distribution of political power, as well as a better functional decentralization of social organization.

Nation-states are realizing that giving up some of their legal prerogatives improves their capacity to meet the changing demands of their societies. Strengthening international organization not only increases the constraints but also the ability of governments to carry out their responsibilities.

Institutional Services

The purpose of an international organization is to provide services both to its members individually and to the world as a whole. Intergovernmental institutions promote national interests by coordinating them into mutually inclusive goals. This process of transforming partial into common interests involves the creation of shared values and norms.

The normative function of international institutions is so important that we shall devote the next section to it. At this point, we can simply mention the direct relationship between common values and international law. Effective legislation correlates with common values to such an extent that any social system must either have shared norms or impressive power to enforce its rules. Since internalized values are preferable to external force, the creation of a global society is better done by multinational organization than superpower imperium.

Global interdependence makes it almost impossible for any significant national policy not to interfere with the policies of other states. It seems that, no matter what a state does, its action will affect some other state. Under the circumstances, friction of policies and conflict of laws among national jurisdictions can only be prevented or at least minimized by international consultations and mutual compromises.

The process of collective policy-making in international institutions requires the active participation of its membership; states are involved in intergovernmental decision-making in order to influence the final outcome. Inter-Governmental Organizations (IGOs) provide the structure in which states interact and conflicting national policies are reconciled. In this way, states affected by the actions of others get a chance to shape the decisions that authorize these actions.

Another advantage of IGO is its relative objectivity in dealing with its members. This impartiality and independence from national interests make these institutions well suited for collective problem solving and peaceful settlement of disputes. Obviously, in their present state, international structures such as the UN fall short of their potential utilization. In order to increase their neutrality these bodies must be given direct sources of funds. Taxing TNCs and licensing the exploitation of international territories would provide more than adequate financing to guarantee the independence of world institutions.

Only such independence will ensure the supremacy of the common interests of mankind over the vested interests of the powers that be. Most important, an international ecosociety would best come about by the concerted efforts of strong international institutions which are not dominated by any single superpower.

International Conservation

As mentioned above, building an ecosociety in one country would be very tenuous without a parallel movement of global scale Although at the beginning, ecopolicies might be initiated by individual nations; at some point, they must be taken up by international institutions if they are to be carried deeper and wider. Only international institutions can coordinate the complex activities and policies of an international ecosystem which would have the support of all nations.

In order to move in that direction, the collective policies of the world will have to balance the economic growth of the underdeveloped countries with the quality of life of the overdeveloped ones; as well as the population decline of the former with the consumption decrease of the latter. In other words, international organization will have to combine the values of a new ecologic order with the goals of a new economic order.

The primary and ultimate goal of the new order would be to establish a global agency to plan and control the impact of technology on the ecology An integral and balanced development of the world requires systemic planning and controlling; anything else will widen the gaps between the rich and the poor and threaten to destroy the ecosystem. The United Nations Conference on Environment and Development (UNCED), which took place in Rio (1992), has been a milestone in this direction. If at least some of the proposals in its Agenda 21 are implemented, the world will be on the road to sustainable development.

Stabilizing the growth patterns suitable for each society means: transferring assets, controlling trade, and generating new sources of investment. The proper exploitation of internationalized spaces by the world institutions should make equalization payments to the poorer regions without undue disturbance of the richer. Bilateral foreign aid can never accomplish such capital transfers without excessive economic burdens or political strings attached to the transaction.

Since it is neither desirable nor possible for the whole world to follow western industrial patterns, the underdeveloped regions must be encouraged not to repeat the mistakes of the overdeveloped. International institutions must therefore emphasize regional development based on: 1) appropriate technology; 2) land reform; 3) practical education; 4) decentralized self-reliance; and 5) autonomy of action within collective decision-making. The economies of most societies should thereby evolve towards small-scale, non-violent efficiency and simplicity, thus, avoiding the massive, wasteful and destructive industrial gigantism of the Northern world.

International institutions can be the intermediaries between different techno-economic systems in order to sanitize and adapt transactions between them from contaminating each other's cultures. This perhaps could become the most significant function of international organization in the process of world conservation.

Universal Values

The complex structural reorganization of the world must be correlated with the universalization of new values. Social institutions have to be synchronized with socio-natural ideals as well as with techno-economic infrastructures. In order to change the international system, we need a new paradigm, or world view, which will appeal to people at large and at the same time coincide with the changing environmental realities. Building such a new mentality is the ultimate problem of international education. For this reason, it was left as the last topic of this chapter; so we now consider the natural and moral values which support a global ecosociety.

Towards a Cosmic Ideology

Building an ecosociety by political action, rather than by natural force or military power, means convincing people of the necessity and desirability of social change. This process involves public consciousness raising by improving people's sense of awareness and increasing their community involvement.

So far, of course, community for most people has been their tribe, region or, at most, nation. Presently, however, the global-village syndrome extends the sense of community to encompass the whole world. A new vision of a global community, founded upon a holistic-futuristic perspective, is presently inspiring different people to work together to change the world. The new universal ideology is drawn from different regions and religions, so its components are transideological and multicultural, emphasizing the shared ideals of mankind and minimizing their differences.

A world ideology does not need uniform values for every aspect of life; a modicum of common ideals suffice to ensure the survival of humanity, while leaving other cultural values to develop separately. Ecological imperatives dictate certain universal values for all mankind, without forcing extreme cultural uniformity. The goal is to promote the proper values and instill the necessary constraints upon human behavior by internalizing the forces of self-control. Only time will show whether most people, who are already overtaxed by the contradictions of their divided loyalties, can accept yet another claim of such remoteness and abstraction as a cosmopolitan ideology.

Permanent Human Values

Although man cannot live by bread alone, he must have bread in order to live at all. The imperatives of physical existence, necessarily form the basic human values upon which all others rest. The primordial value of life *per se* implies the need for a proper nutrition and protection, as well as the right mixture of activity and rest. As the *Universal Declaration of Human Rights* states: everyone has a right to a standard of living adequate for health, which includes food, clothing, housing, medical care and social services.

The human organism can only exist within the narrow ranges of these values; extremes of satiation or deprivation ruin its health and threaten its life. The first duty of society is to determine the proper range of human consumption and production, beyond which nobody should be allowed to either rise or fall.

Once these basic needs of life are provided, we can raise the question of higher values which make life worth living. The necessary material values must be supplemented with desirable spiritual ideals which are equally indispensable to a fully human life. These values include such experiences as love, beauty, and happiness. Complete fulfillment is a combination of both physical and metaphysical value realization. The optimal proportion of the two kinds of values should satisfy the needs of the body as well as those of the mind.

Anything else creates an imbalance which if it gets caught up in a positive feedback can destroy not only individual lives but may prove socially suicidal. This is precisely what is happening both within particular societies and the world in general. The growing disequilibria between ephemeral goods and permanent values, between culture and nature, as well as among human societies, have destabilized personal, social, and ecological systems.

The human community is a complex system interlinked both within itself and its environment. This internal and external linkage must be balanced in the long run, either by natural laws or human values. In order to avoid natural catastrophe, social values must emphasize:

1) naturalistic ethic of respect for the entire ecosystem;
2) globalistic consciousness for an inclusive world community;
3) futuristic orientation that identifies with following generations.

These three principles aim at a balance between the integrity of every biological and sociological entity, as well as the integration of all within the planetary ecosystem. Only such balance avoids the excesses of unsustainable modes of production, unhealthy patterns of consumption and unjust methods of distribution.

Cosmopolitan Morality

Morality is a code of social relationships according to which one's decisions are made only after the wishes of others have been taken into account. To be applied in the level of the world society, morality would mean that the members of the international system consider each other before they formulate their policies. More specifically, no state may act before it calculates the effects that its actions might have on others. Every policy-maker must put himself in the position of those whom his policies might affect. Otherwise, one would be acting unilaterally and egotistically, hence, unethically.

The principle of duly sympathetic consideration not only of our fellow men but the environment should replace irresponsible policies towards both. This principle is no longer merely an ethical ideal to be paid lip service and then ignored for practical purposes. It is by now becoming a realistic prerequisite of international behavior, which is not only politically viable, but absolutely essential for the development of the global community.

A modicum of international *empathy* is the *sine qua non* of any movement towards a transnational ecosociety. In order to reverse the detached policies of "grow-and-let-grow," the world has to act together in concert. This does not mean the abolition of the nation-state, rather its subordination to the global good or the collective exercise of sovereignty.

Once the interdependence of the world is recognized, one has no choice but to cooperate. The dictum "either we live together, or die separately" was never truer than now. In order to apply the principles of consideration and cooperation, states have already increased their consultative activities. Sympathetic consultation, rather than antipathetic confrontation, harmonizes national policies towards more preventive and prescriptive actions. Multilateral exchange of information and positions in a empathetic atmosphere, thus improve international understanding and increase state responsibility.

A responsible state ensures that its activities do not cause damage to other states nor deteriorate the environment as a whole. When national governments are accountable to each other, they adopt complementary policies without a world super-state to impose them. The autolimitation that comes by enlightened self-interest and community spirit balances global necessities with national needs. In this way, it is possible to maintain a decentralized world and at the same time develop a single world ecosociety.

Policy Principles

If the necessity for human values and international ethics is admitted, then we must specify the components of these principles in so far as the ecosociety is concerned. For any ecopolicies to be effective in the world level, there has to be a consensus on the criteria of international stratification: that is, the allocation of differential rewards and the distribution of legitimate powers. Subsequently, it is necessary to mobilize a movement of consensus-building that converges different preferences into more compatible channels.

This convergence will require a change of present values and a reform of existing institutions. Four inter-related processes seem to be necessary for this transformation: 1) cultural convergence; 2) value building; 3) consensus mobilization; and 4) structural reform. In short, the prerequisite for a unified international policy is a certain commitment to a world community.

Resource conservation and environmental preservation are not the only values of the world. Of at least equal priority are those of peace and justice, security and freedom. Policies for environmental rehabilitation and energy conservation, go along with policies to minimize large-scale organized violence and maximize socio-economic well-being. Control of production and consumption cannot be attempted without a parallel equalization of distribution and realization of fundamental human rights.

Accordingly, respect for the natural environment is developed together with respect for human dignity. From this position flows a responsibility to act positively in letting both nature and people help themselves. Our interdependence with nature and each other demands an ecological stable-state and a social-wealth distribution. The new principle of natural equilibrium and human justice abhors imbalances of any kind –whether in space, time or energy.

The problems of war, poverty, injustice, depletion, and pollution, demand systemic and systematic action. In that case, global objectives must aim at peaceful coexistence among many distinct socio-cultural entities which decide their policies collectively. Whatever public issues arise from this process can then be resolved by amicable consultation resulting in consensus and disputes can be settled peacefully through compromise or conciliation. Such emphasis on preventive policies and proactive planning would then minimize natural and social crises and increase our collective capacity to improve the world, rather than merely to survive. Only under these conditions will an ecosociety be either possible or desirable.

* * *

In this Part Two of the book, we tried to juxtapose the consumer life styles dominating some parts of the world with the widespread misery plaguing the rest. Yet, social interdependence tends to blur the boundaries between the individual and the collective, the particular and the universal, the contingent and the perennial. Therefore, in the tightening world system, most dichotomies: national-international; public-private; political-technical; are useful only for academic purposes.

This tells us that the multiple crises of over-consumption by some, and under-nourishment of others; depletion of resources and underdevelopment; environmental pollution and population explosion; cannot be treated separately. Any of these critical problems along with stagflations, famines, epidemics, wars and revolutions threaten to disintegrate the world system by the next century, if we fail to cope with all of them simultaneously.

Some pessimistic scenarios of the future have been constructed, according to which narrow interests and outdated politics of despair in this decade would degrade the world. If these trends continue unabated, the turn of the century will witness the politics of desperation, in which the rich try to keep their wealth by stealth and the poor try to take it by violence. Further deterioration would impose upon the following decades the politics of catastrophe, whereby environmental collapse would meet social decay. The third millennium could then usher in an era of annihilation, combining natural entropy with cultural chaos.

One does not have to believe these apocalyptic prophecies in order to appreciate the seriousness of the situation. It does not take great intelligence to realize that ever expanding wants increases dependence upon natural resources and social systems alike, promoting insecurities and tensions which then break out in violent conflicts.

Once we accept that material expansion cannot be sustained indefinitely, the choice boils down to either waiting for a natural collapse to end the growth, or willing to wind it down it in a gradual, planned and humane manner. The difference in this alternative is basically the human element: whether humans have free will and can consciously choose their fate, or they are merely determined by external forces beyond their control. In any case, to admit to despair is to convert the probability of disaster into a certainty. One must cling to hope and act against the accumulating evidence of cosmic doom.

From this situational analysis, we must conclude that the current crises are neither local nor temporary; therefore partial short-term solutions are not only futile but counterproductive. Lasting solutions are be both global and radical, in that they must change both values and structures of the international system. Moreover, the changes must be brought about by consensual methods as soon as possible. Any further delay in developing a unified global strategy will not only be costly for us but fatal for the next generation.

It is true that voluntary renunciation of the values of growth and selfishness demands an enlightenment and broad-mindedness that is unparalleled in history. But, for the first time, humanity possesses a powerful combination of knowledge, tools, and resources, which should be sufficient to solve its problems; if only we decide upon common goals and generate the will-power to attain them. A top priority is to identify meaningful thresholds of human activity in relation to the capacity of the ecosystem to support them.

Instead of wasting our lives in numb desperation and self-gratification, we could search our imagination and strengthen our resolve to get out of the dead-end road that leads to a mechanical existence for some and no existence for others. We could develop our social nature by cooperating to reverse the present trends which follow from our traditional priorities of economic growth, standard of living, and competitive rewards.

The emerging future society differs both from the natural animism of preindustrial and the artificial mechanism of industrial systems. Instead of choosing between externalities or commonalities, it would focus on interpersonal relations. After conquering nature, the last frontier for humanity is the control of man himself. Self-control and concern for others will be our ultimate claim to civilization.

What we are proposing is that human power must be brought to bear upon history, in order to change its course of events. Our social and political institutions should cooperate to minimize uncertainty and expand the range of our alternatives. The world needs a new natural and social contract between the global policy-makers and the masses of the earth, according to which social justice comes first, followed by quality of life, as well as a steady-state economy and ecology.

The policy-sciences can contribute to this effort by translating policy plans into a social awareness leading to political action. The politics of reform require the creation and activation of innovative groups who identify their interests and aspirations with the new goals, thus pressuring the rest of society to move in that direction.

Bringing about social change is a process which combines human organization and natural resources. Moving from the consumer towards a conserver society, first in postindustrial countries and then in the whole world, requires tremendous resources of both human and natural energies which no one possesses in abundance. It is for this reason that systemic changes can only come about either by cataclysmic forces or collective action. Leaders can only put their ideas into practice by the cooperation of their followers as well as the consent of other groups. Without such horizontal and vertical consensus, any significant goals, such as the ecosociety, are bound to fail.

In this respect, a few progressive people and countries in the world may hold the catalytic key that unlocks the gates of world change. Brute power is neither necessary nor desirable to shift the gears of the global system. What is needed is the right leverage and the sufficient will to pull it. Given the proper means, motive and opportunity, a dedicated group or state can carry the process of reform, even if it is by an example of innovative social policies. In this fast-moving world, one must act quickly; if we fail to exercise our options now, we may never get another chance.

By a proper and timely intervention, concerned people could contribute to shifting the present troublesome trends towards a more agreeable world. If we promote proposals which raise the awareness of people as well as the consciousness of states to the necessity for change, then they will join the movement towards an ecosociety. Once this attempt succeeds, the next step would be to mobilize both subnational and transnational action in the attainment of the new values. With sufficient response and collective effort, the next century should see the transformation of the world into the desired society in which global institutions develop and apply the policies of ecological humanism.

Some people might consider such optimistic scenario as highly idealistic and utopian; but very often what appears to be impractical is due to lack of imagination and determination. It would be tragic if the inertia of apathy or the reaction of cynicism is allowed to carry us to perdition. Everyone must act decisively to identify social problems, clarify public issues, build consensus, and finally carry out the resulting collective will. We could then measure our worth by our endeavors to advance natural conservation, social organization and human civilization.

PART THREE

TECHNOSOCIETY

CHAPTER FIVE

Technopolitics

Telecommunitary Democracy

An important reason for the malaise of modern times, pointed out in the previous part, is the impotence people feel as they are overshadowed by big and powerful institutions. As social structures become larger and stronger, individuals feel smaller and weaker. These feelings of personal worthlessness lead to social alienation and eventually to grave political repercussions.

When people get an inferiority complex, they neither try to control their lives, nor take responsibility for the consequences of their actions. This withdrawal comes at the same time as governments get more involved in social activities and acquire greater impact on people's lives.

These opposing tendencies — disengagement of the individual from public affairs and interference of the state in social life — create the danger of totalitarian elitism, in which a small minority tries to control all aspects of society. Such situation is helped by the advances of technology which make it easier to centralize control and manipulate the masses.

If we are to avoid further deterioration of this situation and reverse the recent trends, we must strengthen our confidence in people and restore the citizen's faith in politics. It is the premise of this chapter that increased politicization decreases alienation and makes far more responsible and legitimate government.

This ideal can now be approximated by applying the new information and communication technologies to enhance the power of the people in public affairs. This utilization of appropriate technology will modernize the political system and bring its outdated nineteenth-century techniques to the twenty-first-century realities.

This process of political development leads to what we term *Telecommunitary Democracy* (TCD). Our thesis here is that TCD is the alternative to technocracy for postmodern societies and the antidote to apathy and anomy.

In order to explain this thesis in as clearly and systematically as possible, we perform a dichotomous analysis. First, conceptualize our terms of reference and setting up the structural elements our system in the sections which cover the concepts, actors and arenas of TCD. Second, animate the system and outline its operation in the sections which deal with the inputs, throughputs and outputs of the TDC political process.

Concepts

We begin with the conceptualization of Telecommunitary Democracy as a political system. In order to do that we first consider the problematic situation that TCD is called upon to correct and then look at the possible means by which such corrective may come about. This initial diagnosis and prognosis sets the tone for the formal definition of TCD.

Political Underdevelopment

In the world of dramatic events and rapid changes in which we live, the astute observer is struck by the magnitude of problems human communities are facing. What is significant about most of these problems is that they are of our own making and thereby could be solved by human intervention. For such solutions to come about, however, it would take great collective effort which the present social systems seem unable to muster. This situation of institutional inadequacy to resolve social issues in order to attain collective goals may be termed *political underdevelopment*.

One hears these days a lot about underdevelopment, but hardly in this context. Underdevelopment, of course, may occur in different contexts; and it is by no means certain that underdevelopment in one area, such as economy, coincides with underdevelopment in another, such as polity. In any case, our concern here centers on the latter concept which has been rather neglected in the contemporary debate.

In addition to economic, the world seems to be suffering from political underdevelopment, a much more insidious disease and harder to diagnose. Yet, like all pathologies, it is a state of functional abnormality which makes a system relatively inefficient and ineffective. Underdevelopment is such a condition of below average performance.

Since politics is a purposeful activity, the inability to perform its task adequately would indicate some kind of underdevelopment, whose symptoms may be found in extreme deviations from normal functions. In that sense there is such thing as over as well as underdevelopment.

Whenever such extremes occur in the body politic, we either have anomy or apathy, depending on whether dialectic participation is too great or too little. Whenever they occur in the state organs, we encounter either absolutism or anarchism, depending on whether there is too much or too little cybernetic control. It may also be that too much dialectics and too little cybernetics coincide to produce anomy and anarchy at the same time, thus compounding the political diseases of social systems.

Since reaching and maintaining a delicate equilibrium is rather difficult, most political systems are in various degrees underdeveloped, so it behooves us to see how we can contribute to their evolution.

The first step in this task is to make quite explicit what is meant by political development, which is to say: the process of improving the capability of a social system to attain its goals by increasing collective decision-making. This definition combines the concepts of *politics* as a dialectic activity of public policy-making and *development* as a cybernetic process of potential-actualizing.

In this sense, a politically developed system would display the opposite traits from those mentioned above, that is empathy, equity, civility, legitimacy. At the core of these traits are the rights and duties of all citizens to participate in the public affairs of their community. This notion of *citizenship* as active role playing in the political arena is the essence of classical politics, but has unfortunately been downgraded in modern times.

The main justification for this *apoliticization* has been the practical impossibility of *direct* involvement of all citizens in the mass societies of millions of people. As a result, the best system that could be devised was *representative democracy*; which in any case is likely to be found more in theory than in practice. It may be, however, that certain technological advances have made further political development a distinct possibility in the foreseeable future. As we see presently, the latest information and communications technology can contribute in developing a society's political as well as economic or cultural aspects.

Information Society

The extraordinary innovations of technology in our generation are having such radical impacts on the contemporary world that they have been compared with the effects of the agricultural and industrial revolutions in the history of mankind. It is said that at present we are undergoing a "third wave" of social change brought about by the *technological revolution* which is transforming the industrial into information societies.

In this postindustrial world, it is the manipulation of information, rather than of matter or energy, that constitutes the principal activity of most people. Eventually, most production of goods and services can be done by robots, leaving humans free for the higher pursuits of knowledge and expression. The technosociety is, therefore, characterized by a high degree of:

a) *Leisure,* due to the automation of manual labour;
b) *Affluence,* due to optimal utilization of natural resources;
c) *Education,* due to the computerization of knowledge;
d) *Community,* due to the communication of information.

Technology is able to handle the constraints of time and space, as well as matter, energy and information. It is, after all, these perennial parameters which, among other things, limit the political activities of most people throughout history. The obstacles to direct democracy have been too much work, poverty, ignorance and isolation. Little wonder that under such conditions, in Hobbe's words, "the life of man was solitary, poor, nasty, brutish, and short."

Of course, one must be careful not to fall into the trap of *technologism*, according to which all problems can be solved by a technological fix. Technology is not a panacea to transform hell into heaven; but it can help along the development process, if properly used. It is with this proviso and conscious of its limitations, that we speak of the social potential of technology.

So far the impact of technology on society has by no means been all positive. The applications of technology have affected some sectors of society (economy) much more than others (polity). For example, the gains of technology in the above four areas have not been translated into the political domain.

As a result, leisure coexists with unemployment, affluence with malconsumption, education with misinformation, and communication with triviality. These technology created contradictions have produced educated and available people who do not know how to use their knowledge and time in a constructive way. It is our major thesis here that as people become more interdependent, informed, affluent and available, they want to participate in public life. If the political system does not provide such outlet, these people become frustrated, alienated and may end up either apathetic or nihilistic.

The great political challenge of our times is to find a way of channelling the extra energy, time, knowledge, and contacts of people in a purposive direction. The answer proposed here is to develop an appropriate political technology to help solve these rising problems of the information society. If not, a likely alternative is the *technocratic* solution which restricts politics within a small scientific elite. In order to avoid that fate, we must promote the *democratic* option.

Tele(Communitary) Democracy

Paraphrasing Lenin's famous dictum, Horacio Godoy equated democratic development to popular power plus technology. We would like in turn to amend this formula in order to fit it to our thesis in the following manner: political development + information technology = teledemocracy. We feel that this new formulation does justice both to Lenin and to Godoy, bringing up to date this succinct equation.

By combining the main notions of the two preceding sections, we have implied both the possibility and desirability of a new type of democratic system. It is felt that high technology can now make possible, what was for so long merely desirable. As such, we postulate that the necessary and sufficient causes of teledemocracy are the application of appropriate technology to the dynamics of political development. Another way of putting it is to say that the goal of political development in an information society is a teledemocracy.

In explaining this principle, we must first define the neologism telecommunitary as the characteristic of an extended community which is held together by the extensive use of telecommunications. The main unifying forces of a telecommunity are telecommunications, whose content is information. Hence, the direct relationship between the information society and telecommunity.

The reason for such use of communication facilities is to allow as large a number of people to exchange information as possible, something which could not be done otherwise. Obviously, such technology must be two-way (interactive), as is the telephone —television has not yet reached this stage to any large extent— so that people can respond to each other.

A combination of all the electronic media can sustain a telecommunity in the tens or hundreds of thousands of people. This is a distinct advance over the number of people who must come together in physical proximity in order to communicate, as was the case in the classical Greek polis or the traditional town meeting. But the main advantage of telecommunications is that they allow the community to exist with little regard to the limitations of space. It is in this sense that Marshal McLuhan spoke of the emerging "global village."

Taking advantage of this technology, political systems can become more "democratic", by which we mean get more people involved in collective decision-making. Since democracy is a system of government controlled by a consensus of its citizens, communication technology can help democracy by facilitating consensus-building among large numbers of people. Together with computers and other information-treating devises, telecommunications can form a systemic network permeating society and democratizing politics.

In this context, the function of technology is to provide information to the citizens so that they can participate intelligently in the policy-making process. Since enlightened decision-making is impossible without information and interpersonal influence is equally impossible without communication, political activity, which depends on both, can only be enhanced by interactive technology.

It is possible to construct a telecommunitary model which optimizes democracy by using state of the art technology. Moreover, it must be emphasized, such technology does not necessarily depend on the degree of industrial development of a society. As mentioned before, political development is not linearly correlated with economic development. The so-called "underdeveloped" countries can benefit directly from high technology in this respect. By the use of a "leap frog" strategy, preindustrial societies could become postindustrial without going through the industrial stage.

In what follows, we present the conditions under which a politically developed system, such as teledemocracy, can operate and on that basis judge its feasibility in the real world.

Actors

Having defined the subject of this study, we now proceed with an examination of its components. Since we deal with a political system, the main elements composing it are its members and their relationships. In this section, we concentrate on the members, who are in effect the people, or more precisely the citizens of teledemocracy. For political purposes, these people operate in groups of various types, the most important of which can be classified under three headings.

Officials

All political systems beyond the very primitive level have an identifiable *government* structure. Government provides the *cybernetic* mechanism of the system by preparing, formalizing and implementing public policies. Government institutions are specialized parts of the political system which try to regulate the dynamics, not only of the political system itself, but of its larger social environment.

Since we assumed that TCD can only exist in a political system which is sufficiently developed, the government must be representative of and accountable to the citizens. As such, a government exists to serve the interests of its society as presented through various political groups. In a politically developed system, such representation should be as accurately reflective of the interests of as many people as possible.

Government is made up of people who act in the name of other people. Government officials act as agents of society at large, but they also acquire interests of their own and interpret the interests of others as they see fit. The resulting conflict of interests may be kept within bounds by various checks and balances, both within government and between government and the rest of the political system.

Within government, the major checks operate usually among different official structures, the most important of which are the legislative and administrative. Legislators are normally elected representatives of geopolitical groups and form the highest authority of the political system. All authoritative policies or laws must be formally approved by the proper legislative bodies which may be assemblies, parliaments, senates, councils, cabinets, committees, conventions, boards and other similar collectivities. Legislators are politicians par excellence, because they occupy central points in the political arena and mediate between the citizens and the administrators.

These latter officials are usually appointed civil servants who run the everyday affairs of government, whereas legislators number in the hundreds, administrators total in the thousands or more. To this quantitative advantage, they also have a qualitative advantage of specialization and expertise; therefore, they form quite a formidable group in all advanced political systems. They not only interpret and execute public policies, but also initiate, prepare, plan and recommend alternatives to the other groups of the political system. Their influence is considerable in all stages of the decision-making and implementing process.

These two groups of government officials sometimes work in concert, other times in conflict, but in any case, their contributions in the political system are indispensable. As we see later on, they play a crucial role in the functioning of any polity, including TCD.

Citizens

At the other end of the political structure from that of the government is the *public*. This large group of people comprises nominally all the citizens of the community. In reality only those people who have some involvement and influence in policy-making count in any significant sense. Unfortunately, this group of people is a very small proportion of the public (usually less than 10%). An important task of political development is to increase this ratio as much as possible by politicizing more and more people.

One index of the influence of the people at large is *public opinion* as measured in polls and other surveys. Voting at elections or referenda is a formal way of measuring public opinion towards particular people or issues. Such measures, however, are few and far between; normally public opinion is vaguely expressed and impressionistically noted. Another index of political development would be to make such articulations and measurements more accurate and more often.

As mentioned previously, the reasons for the low involvement of citizens in the political system and, hence, the difficulty in expressing their opinions, are related to the low feasibility of such undertaking due to physical and technical constraints. Theoretically, most systems approve of the desirability of increased involvement, but in practice very few do anything about it. In this case, TCD can at least overcome the technical obstacles of these aspects of political development.

There are other aspects, nevertheless, which are harder to deal with. So far we spoke of the public as a large undifferentiated mass. This is only partly true, since the public is ultimately composed of individuals. But the other side of the coin is that individuals rarely operate alone in politics. In order to multiply their influence they coalesce in groups and act through them.

Significant groups in the political system are parties, associations, corporations, movements, factions, caucuses, societies, clans and other similar affinity sets, which crystalize positions and mobilize actions. Each of these brings together people who share a particular opinion or interest which they protect and promote in the political system or more particularly in the government.

Of course, groups like individuals are not all equal; some are more powerful than others. Their political influence varies according to the number of members they represent or the amount of resources they dispose. In most cases, a few of these groups can bring to bear inordinate influence and so dominate decision-making. These groups may represent certain classes (bourgeois), professions (military), regions (Northerners), and other such conglomerations, effectively exclude others from participating in the political process.

This centralization and monopolization of power is a characteristic of political underdevelopment and must be reversed if a TCD is to function properly. In that case, influence will have to be more evenly distributed among these groups and eventually among citizens in general. The spread of influence, whether in individuals or groups, is directly proportional to the spread of participation throughout the membership of the political system. It is in this task of extending the participatory activity of the public that we now introduce a third class.

Mediators

Interposed between the government and the public, there are placed certain people whom we call mediators, because they facilitate the contacts not only between these two great sectors but within them as well. This third sector or estate shares some characteristics of the other two and is in the best position to perform a mediatory function in the TCD.

The essence of this sector is the production and distribution of information, so the people in it are experts in manipulating and communicating knowledge. Although this sector exists in every social system, it is most developed in information societies, as we have explained in the first chapter. The reason is that technological advances have made it possible to accumulate and spread great quantities of information to the public at large.

The actors in the mediating sector may be divided into two types depending on their primary function. In the first group belong the producers or transformers of knowledge. These people comprise many professions and specialities such as researchers, scientists, inventors, programmers, consultants, statisticians and other similar occupations. The influence of these actors is based on their knowledge and the use they make of it in society. Knowledge can be easily translated into power because it is necessary for effective decision-making and implementation.

Complementing the professionals of the above type is another class of occupations dealing with the communication of information. These people include such specialists as journalists, publishers, messengers, teachers, advertisers and broadcasters. The numbers in these occupations have been and will be steadily increasing along with their influence in the policy-making process. For this reason, they are at the heart of any TCD.

Information and communication workers try to fulfill the growing need of complex systems for knowledge. As societies develop they process more and more information which is required for increasingly sophisticated activities. The most political of these activities is the decision-making process, so *informediators* become indispensable brokers in politically developed systems.

In order to classify the positions all these groups occupy in relation to each other, we constructed the structural diagram which appears at the end of this section. The diagram illustrates what has been said and summarizes the relationships of the principal actors of a TCD. It should serve as a synoptic picture of the structure of a developed political system.

This system is represented by a pentagon, divided into two opposing parallelograms at its sides and an inverted triangle in the middle, representing the three sectors of TCD. As is the case with any model, this illustration simplifies reality down to what we consider its most essential components: the cast of characters and their relationships.

The six types of actors are clearly distinguished in the diagram (two in each sector) by the shaded circles. As we have described them in this chapter, each of these circles represents one of the TDC estates, within which are to be found many political groups. The position that these groups occupy in the system are shown to be equivalent, except for the communications estate which is our protagonist.

The choice for the central focus highlights the importance of informediation in our scheme of things. The main communication channels (represented by unidirectional lines) pass through the area of these key actors. In effect, they are the gatekeepers of the information-flow in the whole system. Since they control the flow of such important resources, they in turn must be effectively monitored by the system, perhaps more than any of the other groups.

Using advanced computer and communications technology, TCD structures should be able to handle the increased information necessary for better decision-making. More important for politics is that technology would permit the treatment of larger inputs from more people, thus democratizing the public policy-making process.

Techno-Political System

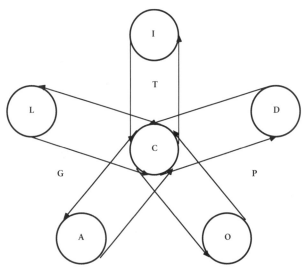

LEGEND		
Legislation	Communication	Demos
Administration	Information	Organization
Government	Technology	Public
L+A=G	C+I=T	D+O=P

TELEDEMOCRACY MODEL

Arenas

The structural model used in the preceding section focused on the major actors of TCD and their relationships, without regard to the *geopolitical* level of their position. It is now time to take this factor into account by introducing various arenas of political activity. In this way, we combine both horizontal and vertical dimensions to our analysis. In the following sections, the discussion therefore deals with the three most significant levels of public policy-making.

Local

The local level is the primary arena of politics. It is here that the ordinary citizen has the greatest chance of direct influence on events. Local politics are fundamental to a TCD. A political system cannot develop without a strong basis on local institutions. It is necessary to build such grass root structures to ensure popular participation in public affairs.

Traditionally, the arena of local politics is a *community* defined in geographical terms, such as neighborhood, ward, county, municipality, constituency or region. Historically, this spatial delimitation of the community was based on the constraints of communication beyond a certain distance. With telecommunications this area can be enlarged considerably, so that the main limiting factor becomes the number of people who can communicate with each other directly.

If the primary community is the circle of people who are in direct and continuous communication, then this group is the power base for the exchange of influence. By the use of a personal computer, television and telephone, every citizen can expand the range of his influence in many directions. From this increased communication follows a higher capacity for organization and better coordination for political action.

It seems inevitable that widespread use of communication technology will enlarge the body politic and politicize more people than ever before. Such politicization, however, can threaten political stability, because it increases demands and heightens pressures on the system. To contain this danger, there is need for constraint from all parties, which can only come about by a community-mindedness based on enlightened self-interest.

Responsible citizenship is a function of participation, so that as people become more involved in public affairs; they also become more prudent in their decisions. This tendency, along with a more informed public opinion due to better communications, should combine to improve the quality of political life, as well as increase its quantity. Although little knowledge is a dangerous thing, more knowledge and involvement can provide the antidote.

Strengthening the institutions of community politics must be the first task of TCD. This task will necessitate the decentralization of power, so that the local arena becomes the place where more decisions are taken. Since people will participate in something only if the feel that their time and energy is not wasted, local *autonomy* must be the principle upon which TCD can operate. Technology and politics have to be brought together to ensure an optimal role for the citizen in his community.

National

The central level on which politics is conducted is the national, state or federal, depending on the type of constitution a society has. This is the level where a good part of the sovereignty of the political system resides, so the policies taken are of major importance. It is therefore necessary that decisions made here are as democratic as possible.

It is on the national arena that telecommunications technology can be of the greatest help to politics, because at this level we deal with greater numbers of people over greater distances. The political system here is much more complex and impersonal than at the local level, because it tends to fall into oligarchic modes of decision-making and is prone to loose touch with the individual citizen.

In order to remedy somewhat these dangers, we need numerous strong *intermediating* structures to close the widening gap between the state and its citizens. These structures are public organizations which associate groups of citizens who share a common interest. At the local level, these groups tend to be geopolitical (neighborhood clubs, townhall assemblies, county circles); whereas at the national level, they tend to be affinity groups (professional associations, business organizations, syndicates and specialized societies). The membership of these functional groups is spread over large areas, so telecommunications take on great importance in keeping them in touch with each other.

The structure of TCD outlined in the last chapter is such as to optimize these contacts. The vertical organization of the system should be based on national associations of community groups, so that people would be represented by intersecting memberships in both regional and functional associations. In this way, the various facets of multiple interests found in complex social systems would be adequately reflected in the political system of TCD.

Since TCD would be populated by highly informed people, needs and demands would be much more disaggregated, and response to them will have to be more individualized and particularistic. Informed people tend to be better at organizing themselves to voice their concerns and press for their rights. Collective action increases with information. At the same time, high levels of communication correlate with participation, so that education, organization, and mobilization tend to converge in the same social groups.

Supplementing these interrelated vertical and horizontal structures, there will be a direct channel of communication between the individual and the state through an institutionalized system of *televoting*. Advanced technology can make it possible to take instant public opinion polls on any political issue by supplying each household with a two-way communication facility for this purpose.

Although TCD is a more sophisticated political system than a simple plebiscitary democracy, popular referenda do have a place in it, as long as they operate as complements to group interactions. What is important is that a democracy utilize a variety of multidirectional interactive communication networks to ensure that citizens are given every opportunity to voice their opinions and influence the decisions taken on their behalf by the state.

Global

Nation-states are the principal geopolitical divisions of the world, so that at the international level they are the main actors of the macropolitical system. The structure of that system reflects this reality by the number and variety of intergovernmental organizations, as well as the plethora of diplomatic interactions which are going on all the time.

The decision-making process at this level, although more informal and decentralized, resembles that of the other two levels. With the United Nations system at its center, the international society takes collective decisions and establishes global codes of conduct for its members. Even if the strength of these norms and policies is not always very high, the fact remains that a world political system does exist.

Along with it, there also functions a world communications system through which transborder data flows in increasing quantities. Because of the importance of information for intelligent decision-making, the control of these communication channels has become a highly political issue. Many people believe that both the media and the messages of this international network are unduly controlled by a few biased sources. The call for a New International Communications Order is a demand for a democratization of information exchanges in the world.

In that sense, NICO is the equivalent of TCD in the world scale. At that level, our TDC model will have to be translated in a looser form, but its principles will remain the same. The differences here are that the collective actors represent larger and more heterogeneous groups, such as multilateral diplomatic conferences and the international civil service in the official arena, world public opinion and transnational associations in the unofficial arena, as well as the global communications network and its information resources.

In order to democratize the world political system, the power centers of the international community must be more widely spread throughout its members. This means that the flows of influence in the system should be more extensively distributed and evenly balanced. This goal can be approached with improved communication which will close the gap between information-rich and information-poor countries.

Closing the information-power gap is related to the general North-South dialogues. For the confrontation of these opposing interests to turn into a creative dialectic, there is need for more mediating structures to attenuate contradictions and accommodate conflicts. These mediators should be connected both vertically and horizontally: firstly, by strengthening infra and supra-national institutions, and secondly, by improving public and para-governmental associations.

It seems that, in many respects, the nation-state is too big for certain functions and too small for others. For this reason, it should decentralize to allow more local autonomy in selected areas, at the same time as it increases international cooperation and coordination where necessary. Influence should flow both downwards and upwards from the middle level of the nation-states, as well as towards the peripheries from intergovernmental and transnational power centers.

This exposition of the structures of TCD in the three major arenas of the political system is admittedly very sketchy, but it should give a fair idea of the form and content of our model. Moreover, it shows the requirements of TCD and hints at the gap between them and the present realities. Obviously, this gap is significant, but by no means impossible to bridge, given the continuation of technological advances and a modicum of political will.

By the beginning of the next century, such gradual application may not be as difficult as it seems now. Although working out the development strategy, attaining that goal is not part of this study. So we only touch upon some of its policy aspects in the second half of this chapter dealing with TDC dynamics.

Input Factors

This presentation of the *operational* aspects of the TCD model complements the *structural* components whose description was just completed. The first phase of the operational model involves the various factors which enter the political system as environmental inputs. These factors are, in effect, the needs or wants of the different social actors as they crystalize into political demands and transmit themselves to the public institutions of the system.

In order to clarify this process, we have summarized its steps in the diagram appearing in the next page. This flow chart is the dynamic complement of the structural diagram presented in the previous section. The chart has two dimensions: the vertical, consisting of the six groups of actors introduced in chapter two; and the horizontal, consisting of the sequence of nine steps involved in the political process, grouped in three operational phases.

As was the case with the structure of the TCD model, the process is also centered in the role of the mediating actors. The lines representing relationships in the structural model now become arrows representing a series of events leading to and from the arenas of action of each actor. Each of these centers of activity is represented by an octagon; while the focus of the following explanations will be on the national level.

Political Process Flow Chart

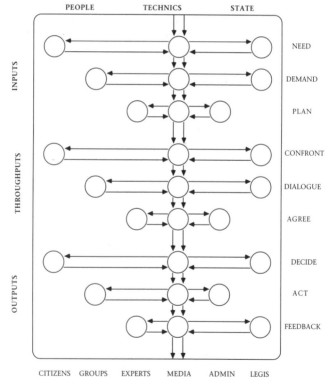

ACTOR-NODES & CHANNEL-PHASES

Human Needs

We chose to begin this inquiry at the *need-determination* stage, because it seems to be a logical point to enter the cycle of political activities. Human needs are the necessities for the existence and development of persons. The fulfillment of these needs is a basic drive for the maintenance and enhancement of life.

Human needs are a political issue in so far as they are subject to interpretation and prioritization. Needs and their subjective translation into wants are a subject of controversy, because they are related to different perceptions of interest. Moreover, opinions as to the best way of fulfilling them differ, so people do not always agree on what they want and how to go about obtaining their desires.

Social institutions help people identify their individual and collective needs and then try to provide the means for fulfilling them. In order to improve the performance of political systems in this domain, TCD relies on the aid of information technology. Such technology can carry out this function in three main political arenas, individual education, public opinion and representative institutions.

As far as the first area is concerned, personal computers and home libraries increase the access to and storage of large amounts of information for the average person. Increased information is the first ingredient to *consciousness-raising* and enables the individual to realize his proper needs. More informed people are in a better position to know their interests and to order their priorities in a more realistic way. As computers become less expensive and more convivial, they spread their capacities for information to more people, creating a more enlightened population.

Supplementing information technology, the mass media help with the communication of information in society. Both electronic and print media bring information to the people and help them find out the opinions of each other. The formulation and accumulation of many points of view add up to public opinion, easily expressed by advanced technology of polling.

More rapid and accurate survey techniques will increase the knowledge of politicians as to what people want. The clearer expression of popular will should make public affairs more reflective and effective. Legislative bodies will be better able to take into account the various shades of opinion of different people and improve their representative capacity.

In all these instances, the role of information and communication technology is crucial. The political system must ensure that this role is performed unhindered and unbiased. These two conditions are necessary to the greatest extent possible, in order to provide the system with reliable and useful information. The technological sector must be both independently run and closely scrutinized to guarantee its quality and impartiality. On that assumption, the first step of the teledemocratic process will be well taken.

Demands

Once needs have been determined, the next step is *demand-articulation*. Needs by themselves are not politically significant until they have been expressed into specific demands upon the government. The translation of needs into demands is very important in public affairs.

The central arenas for such articulation are the various political groups which aggregate individual interests into common positions. As we have mentioned, these groups range from small clubs to large movements and are especially exemplified by political parties. Individuals join or form these groups in order to improve their chances of being heard by strengthening their collective voice.

In order to organize and propagate such groups, people must be in constant communication with each other. Isolated individuals have little political influence, so the power of public opinion alone is too diffused in general to be of much use in specific political decisions. What is necessary to move the system in one direction or another is the concerted collective effort of forceful groups.

Communications technology can help tremendously in keeping people in touch with each other and allow them to find out their common interests. The telephone network plays a primordial role here, because it not only makes it possible for people to talk to each other over great distances, but also interconnects computers and other information facilities. Through it, facts and opinions can be exchanged and actions coordinated, things which are indispensable in politics.

Providing the channels for the flow of information is not the only service the media can supply to the political system. Equally important is their contribution to the content and form that the information takes. It is no secret that the media shape as well as carry messages.

In this respect, the information sector of the system selects, stores, edits, recalls, as well as diffuses and interprets data. The decisions made in each of these activities by certain people promotes some information at the expense of other. Information and communication experts are responsible for both the quantity and quality of facts and opinions circulating in the political system.

Here again, since all people are subjective and biased in translating facts into opinions, the only way to maximize the usefulness of information is to let as many opinions be expressed as possible. In this instance the worst thing for the political process would be a monopoly of information sources and communication facilities. The information market place must be kept as open and the communication channels as unobstructed as possible.

In this way politicians will get a better sense of the demands made upon them by the various interest groups in the system. The accurate transmission of the extent and direction of these demands determines the overall pressure put upon the political system at any given time. Attention will obviously be given to the sources which can exert the greatest pressures as they are transmitted through the media to the proper response centers.

Plans

The third factor entering the political process in the TCD model is the way needs and demands are analyzed and the responses to them are prepared. The pressures upon the political system trigger certain activities in various public institutions. These activities aim to understand the meaning of the pressure and plan the proper reaction to it.

Explaining social events and their impact upon the political system is a complex and difficult task, which requires experience and expertise. Developed systems train specialists for this purpose as part of their information sectors. These people are research scientists, political analysts, technology assessors, and policy consultants who work in laboratories, think-tanks, universities and similar institutions of higher learning.

Social scientists backed by advanced information technology are now able to process large amounts of data and design sophisticated models simulating the operation of complex systems. The hardware and software utilized in these activities help people clarify their concepts and formulate their problems.

Moreover, various techniques are now developing to systematize the diagnosis and prognosis of social dysfunctions, so that it is easier to prevent rather than react to them. As societies become more complicated, intuitive responses are no longer adequate to solve their problems. More scientific handling of such problems has, therefore, become necessary in a large scale.

The information society produces an increasing number of experts to analyze social demands and recommend appropriate measures to alleviate them. Accordingly, they study the relevant factors and produce alternative ways of handling problems. These studies form part of the inputs to the political system, along with the information about the needs and demands of the people.

The role of the media in this stage is to simplify and publicize these scientific studies and plans, so that people understand their implications. Such publication and interpretation increases the public's perception of its options and thus influences its demands. As a result, it shapes the political agenda of public debate.

The last important group in this process is the civil
service. The government administrators play a facilitating and often decisive role in this respect. They
request and support research, they coordinate various projects and they regulate the activities of the different groups involved in the political system. In this
way, they influence the choice of studies undertaken
and the fate of their results.

A TCD must make sure that the power of the
bureaucracy is kept within bounds by maintaining
independent sources of research and study as well as
of publication and diffusion throughout society. Only
then will the political system receive diverse and balanced information along with analysis and criticism,
thus widening its range of options from which it can
choose the most desirable public policy.

Political Interactions

With this section, we reach the core of politics as a
collective enterprise. It is at this stage where the various input factors just outlined are treated and ultimately transformed into policy outputs. This treatment of the many constants and variables to be taken
into account in any particular case goes through a
series of events. For our purposes, we outline only
three of them, which are deemed especially important.

Confrontation

So far, we have identified the major inputs to the
political system as the demands of various groups.
These demands are presented as social critiques,

interest positions, or policy proposals by their different promoters or adherents. The differing opinions of what should be the means and ends of social activity create public controversy which is fought out in the political arena. *Public issues* are entered in the political agenda for discussion and resolution.

The public confrontation of diverse and opposing views is the preliminary condition of any political activity. Without such confrontation, there would be no politics. In this sense, disagreement is the ground upon which politics flourishes, since the *raison d'être* of the political process is to convert disagreement into agreement.

As a first step, we begin with the existence of divergence of opinion and interest among the various political players who confront each other in the *agora*. These players present, as best they can, their point of view on the social problems to be faced and their suggestions for solving them. The political market-place displays a variety of "goods" which their proponents are trying to "sell" to the public.

The information and communication sector as we saw, play a key role in preparing and presenting these alternatives for public consumption. The function of information experts is to join the public debate for or against particular options, pointing out the advantages and disadvantages of each. In parallel, the function of the communication experts is to publicize these debates and spur public interest in them.

A major goal of TCD thus is to break down wherever possible the separation between political performers and their audiences. Through interactive technology, experts, citizens, and politicians are supposed to exchange information and participate in the *public debate*. The use of open line radio shows, televised panel discussions or parliamentary debates and public meetings, all increase popular involvement in politics.

The question has often been posed as to how much of such political activity can a society take before it becomes too paralyzed or polarized to do anything else. Since politics is a time consuming and labor intensive activity, each social system will have to determine what part of its scarce resources it will devote to politics; TCD has no choice but to put great emphasis on active citizenship as a major responsibility of its members. The conditions in an information society make this involvement not only possible but necessary.

Negotiation

At the same time as all this public debate is going on, another process is developing behind the scenes. As is well known, politics is not merely carried out in open confrontation; more important is what happens below the surface and behind the scenes. These latter activities often give politics its bad name, but are indispensable to its operation. All one can do is make them as accountable to public scrutiny as possible.

Informal and *in camera* politics involve the negotiations taking place among different interest groups in order to arrive at some mutual compromise. Negotiations include the give and take of bargaining where interests are exchanged and deals are struck. These activities determine "who gets what, when and how" or what the costs and benefits of the various options will be for each party.

In this negotiating process, the public debate provides one of the factors. Whoever seems to be convincing more people improves his bargaining power.

As public opinions shift and change, so do the negotiating positions. The number of people behind each interest determines its weight relative to the others.

Of course, other factors enter the political equation in which power is calculated on the basis of what resources one can bring to bear on the issue at hand. It is here that the unequal financial resources of different groups may be decisive in tipping the balance one way or another and making their views prevail both in public and private interactions.

Traditionally, the role of the media in this phase of politics has not been great because of the secrecy surrounding these proceedings. With political development come larger openings which can give the public a better glimpse of the goings on within the inner sanctums of politics. As people become more aware and active, they are no longer content in letting small groups take crucial decisions behind closed doors.

Although the Wilsonian dictum of "open covenants, openly arrived at" cannot be put into practice entirely, the onus has shifted on the secret activities to justify their necessity. The proliferation of the means of communications have shrunk the areas of secrecy and have opened up more and more activities to the light of publicity.

Nevertheless, discrete contacts and negotiations are part of the nature of things and will always be part of politics. Where information technology can help in these matters is to make the power calculus indispensable to negotiations more explicit and accurate. Political consultants can aid interest groups defend their positions and devise game strategies to maximize their gains and minimize their losses.

The manifestations of this bargaining is reflected in the activities of the political system. Thereby the politicians take into account this dialectical process with the exchanges that it produces and the directions that it takes. On the basis of this accounting, they eventually have to choose the winning combination in any particular case.

Accommodation

As is evident by now, politics is not simply the counting of heads to determine a majority for or against a certain position or person. Rather, it is a dialectical activity in which conflicting interests converge towards a common area of agreement. This goal of interest-accommodation through confrontation and negotiation points to the final stage of the political process.

Accommodating diverse and opposing interests is a delicate task which must be carefully carried out in any political system. To do so takes a large measure of good will as well as highly competent people. One must, therefore, find enough willing and able participants to perform this collective search for consensus to its successful conclusion.

Consensus-building is the other side of the political coin from issue-confronting. One comes at the beginning and the other at the end of the political process. According to the model we have been following, political hostilities open when controversies are put in the public agenda and close when they are resolved or postponed. In either case, they follow this cycle of escalation-climax-anticlimax.

In this last stage the function of political agents is to find the common denominator of different positions. It is axiomatic that such common denominator exists underneath even the most contradictory interests, otherwise the social system would break down

This minimal community of interests can be increased by enlightened political activity at the stage of consensus-building.

Unfortunately, in this domain, humanity has not made much progress in the last two thousand years. Consensus-building techniques and political problem-solving methods have remained the same throughout history. It is only now that technological advances have begun to spill over to the political sphere.

Although political technology is still at its infancy, there are areas where much promise is shown in radical breakthroughs. In this area, the electronic *consensor* is such an apparatus which helps the search for collective agreement by instant feedback devises. By extending and perfecting this machine, political groups can improve their capacity for arriving at a consensus.

Research to develop better tools and means of accommodation goes on in many social-science centers. Specialists in this field are increasingly involved in conceiving and applying new techniques of conflict resolution by consultation, mediation and conciliation, as well as negotiation. This development of political technology and methodology is necessary to the existence of TCD and must come about along with it.

Through its civil service, government can promote such process by supporting private initiatives and testing innovative procedures. Specialized public agencies can provide expert mediators and appropriate facilities to enhance the search for a common interest. As they succeed in doing so, the political system becomes more efficient and decision-making that much easier.

Output Production

We have now reached the final stage of the political process where decisions are taken and executed. This last section looks into the decision-making, implementing and evaluating process from the point of view of our model. As is illustrated in the flow chart, this stage includes the outputs of public policy and the application to which they are put. The following points outline the main steps of this sequence of events.

Decision Taking

As mentioned, TCD is neither simply a plebiscitary nor a representative democracy, although it has aspects of both. At the one extreme is a system where citizens themselves formally vote for legislation, whereas the other extreme is a system where citizens only elect the people who legislate on their behalf. Between these two schemes, TCD involves the citizens in the legislative process, but reserves the formal ratification of the law to their elected representatives.

So far, we have seen how the citizens, both individually and collectively, will participate in the shaping of public policy at all the stages of its making, with the help of high technology. This continuous involvement by individuals in the community is necessary for a positive public input into policy-making and not merely *ex post facto* approval or criticism.

By the time, draft legislation has arrived at this advanced stage of decision, it is almost impossible to influence it without a major political crisis. Proper timing is very important in law-shaping. Because of that, a democratic legislative process, unlike crisis management, needs a certain period of time to go through its paces. As such, TCD must be *proactive* rather than reactive, so that it has enough lead-time to prepare to meet upcoming social problems and not chase after them.

All the political system can do at the decision-making stage, after all the public debate and private compromises have been made, is register the final public opinion on the matter. Hopefully, by then the consensus will have emerged or at least a majority for or against the proposed policy. On the basis of this popular will, the formal legislative organs can take their authoritative decision and thus promulgate the new law.

If, on the other hand, the outcome of the political process is inconclusive and significant divisions still remain, the whole thing needs to be rethought and should go back to the drawing board. Politics does not always succeed in reaching collective agreement, which means that this particular issue at hand is not ready for decision and should not be forced through in normal circumstances.

In any case, information and communications technology makes it easier to determine the state of any proposal as it goes through the system and avoids unpleasant surprises at the end. If this political process operates as it should, the outcome of policy proposals would be a foregone conclusion long before they are voted upon by the decision-makers.

Implementation

Although most political activity ends with decision-making, certain political manifestations carry on beyond that stage. Strictly speaking, postdecision stages involve mainly administrative activities which carry out the approved policies. Once the decision has been taken, even those who opposed it are supposed to accept and comply with it.

In reality, controversy may still continue by those who are still opposed to the policy, as well as by those who disagree as to the best way of implementing it. The first group may include powerful people who could sabotage the effectiveness of the policy in many ways along its execution. In this case, there must be adequate public monitoring to overcome these obstacles. The media have a role to play during this state by informing the public of the progress or lack of it in policy-implementation.

In the second case of methodological disagreement, public scrutiny is much more difficult because it would involve high specialization and expertise. Technical or administrative matters of policy-execution must necessarily be left with those responsible for carrying them out. The public or private sector charged with implementation must be given the proper mandate to fulfill its task.

Apart from continuous supervision by independent agencies and periodic verifications or progress reports, the political system must be eternally vigilant to keep executive power accountable to it. The growth of public and private bureaucracies running large and complex socio-economic institutions are in danger of getting out of control. Whether in government or corporation, technocrats tend to operate in secret and independently of adequate political supervision.

Part of this situation, of course, is a necessary evil that comes along with a technological civilization. Nevertheless, it must be kept within bounds by political checks and balances. Technology here can help ameliorate the situation created. Informediation and telecommunication can improve public scrutiny and political control of bureaucratic operations and administrative practices.

In this respect, public institutions would monitor private firms in the execution of public contracts, and private associations would keep an eye on the activities of the civil service. Information and communication experts could mediate between these two main executive sectors.

The knowledge that there is public scrutiny, by itself, prevents overt abuses of executive authority in most cases. But in cases where these do occur, an open system is much more likely to discover these abuses and much easier to correct them. Public exposure of such scandals, provides for periodic cleansing of the system, and is thus a good political cathartic.

Feedbacks

The final steps of the political or any other purposive process are evaluation and feedback. A process which aims to reach some goal must be able to determine if and when the goal has been attained. The implementation process must be evaluated both as to the policy it executed and the strategy it used to do so. For that reason, the political system should devise a means-ends methodology to judge its achievements.

As the name implies, *evaluation* involves values in measuring performance. The values of a political system, being more procedural than substantive, emphasize the way politics operates, more than the policies it produces. Since the purpose of politics is interest-accommodation through dialectical issue-resolution, its evaluation measures the extent to which consensus has been reached and conflict has been resolved. A successful political system should be able to convert controversy into agreement by the exchange of influence.

TCD maximizes its chances of performing these activities by utilizing the latest information and communication technology. Such technology makes it possible to realize TCD's central value of citizen participation in public policy-making. One must be careful to note that politics, in general, and democracy, in particular, cannot guarantee the superiority of its policies over those of other systems. Dictatorships may arrive at some wise decisions as well, but that is beside the point, since they do not do so by the proper procedures.

Nevertheless, a political system must also have standards of evaluation of its policies as well as of their implementation. Policy-evaluation has lately made some progress in becoming more systematic. Expert evaluators are now able to audit program performance by using state of the art techniques. These evaluations must be made public as soon as they are completed, so that discussion on them can be carried out in the community as well as in the legislature and subsequent action taken.

This brings us to the importance of feedback in correcting the faults of the system. The practical purpose of evaluation is to learn the lessons of history, so as not to repeat them. Evaluation in this sense is an *educational* activity, indispensable to the development process. If the political system is to improve, it must find out and correct its past errors.

In this educational task, the information and communication sector is evidently crucial. The people involved in this role must perform constructive criticism and impact-assessment, which should then be diffused throughout the system.

Ultimately, of course, the supreme judge is the public as a whole and especially those who have been affected, either in the cost or benefit side of policy. Since the main aim of public policy is to help fulfill human needs, its success must be judged to the degree that it has done so. If certain needs have been satisfied as a result, then policy has done some good.

Yet, it is well known that as some needs are satisfied others rise to take their place, so the cycle of policy-making never ends. The feedback hopefully serves to improve the next round of political activity, which goes on and on, as long as people disagree on how best to fulfill their perceived needs. Therefore, the outputs of one cycle become the inputs of another and the process repeats itself *ad infinitum.*

The exemplary cycle just completed was hopefully made clear in the preceding flow chart. All the activities mentioned are illustrated on that chart and the formal sequence is shown by the arrows connecting them. The movement of the vectors from left to right measure time, whereas those going up and down measure space.

It should be noted that, although time is unidirectional, the activities along it are not always and necessarily in that order. Reality is much more untidy than its ideal representation. Similarly, the interactions between the various groups and centers of power are not exclusively related as shown but are subject to secondary contacts and partial feedback loops.

All these details could not be shown in this crude diagrammatic representation without rendering it completely incomprehensible. Greater in depth analysis can only be done by focusing on one aspect or phase of this process and magnifying it to see smaller and smaller elements. This magnification could be a sequel to the present study and would require much more work beyond our scope here.

It is expected that by now the form and function of TCD have been sufficiently explained, so as not to require further summarizing. Similarly, both the possibility and desirability of the TCD have been established well enough to allow those interested to move on and consider the most feasible strategy of bringing it about.

Before this is done, however, we conclude by some thoughts on the transition from the present realities to the future ideals. The model of TCD presented here is not so utopian as it may appear at first sight. The world has come a long way in many respects which, if only properly taken advantage of, can move us further in the direction of political development.

The principles enunciated here have already been accepted by the international community. Many institutions of the United Nations System have implicitly or explicitly called for increased popular participation in policy-making as a fundamental aspect of the development process. The 1980 Belgrade Declaration of UNESCO, for example, calls for "respect for the right of the public, of ethnic and social groups and of individuals to have access to information sources and to participate in the communication process." Since then, the political revolutions *circa* 1990 confirmed the trend towards more democratic systems.

Now that these principles have been established and promoted, the next step is to think out their implications and work out their extensions. We must have no delusion that this is an easy task. The inertia of social systems and the vested interests of powerful groups will resist any attempts to do so. Yet the forces of history and the will of people can combine to overcome such resistance.

The consciousness-raising and rising expectations of people everywhere increases social demands and political pressures which cannot be ignored indefinitely. The need for overall development is spreading throughout the world and has to be faced by local as well as global institutions.

As has often been pointed out, development is not necessarily economic growth. More subtle and insidious forms of underdevelopment have to do with lack of information and communication, as well as with exclusion from participation in the decisions which affect one's life. Development beyond a certain minimum threshold must take into account these more complex and intangible human needs.

The development process is not a linear sequence which would limit socio-political development only to those who have gone through a particular kind of economic development. TCD is not to be thought of as a luxury that only the rich can afford, because information and communication technology does not require heavy industrialization. On the contrary, technology can replace much of industry with education. That is why, the control of the media of communication in an information society is as important as the ownership of the means of production in an industrial society.

Because of this potential power of knowledge, we must make sure that it does not become the exclusive domain of very few countries or classes. For that reason, the TDC model advanced here is a viable alternative to such political maldevelopment in local, national or international systems.

CHAPTER SIX

Metapolitics

Defining Political Development

The purpose of this final chapter is to integrate what has been said so far by devising a conceptual definition of *political development*. This phrase combines two different terms, each of which has its own separate meaning. When put together, the question arises as to their combined sense: is there such a thing as political development? Or is this combination nonsensical?

It is such questions which largely belong to metapolitics, so our discussion here may be properly called metapolitical. On that basis, we consider the deeper meaning of politics, both in its etymological and epistemological sense. Once this is done, one can then apply that meaning in either conceptual or empirical contexts.

As the lengthy bibliography at the end of the book indicates, political development has been used extensively in the recent literature of political and social sciences. Yet a perusal of these sources shows that its meaning is still moot. Each author uses the term in his own way which suits a particular purpose. No one has presented a rigorous definition of this complex concept; therefore it means different things to different people. So much so, that this situation of so many disparate and contradictory definitions has led some critics to call for the demise of political development as a useful concept.

That would indeed be one solution by elimination. Yet, we live in an era in which the process of "devel-

257

opment" dominates the thoughts, if not the actions, of many people. Moreover, one of the two principal axes of international politics revolves around the so-called North-South confrontation. The well-known dichotomy of the contemporary world into more and less developed countries (DCs and LDCs) is a case in point which underlines the importance placed on this concept.

In general, "development" is used in the sense of "economic". This qualification of development, most of the times left unsaid, restricts the concept to a process related with industrialization. In this sense, "economic development" can mean a very specific thing, but the various interrelations with this process could not avoid a certain spill-over into other areas.

As a result, we have social, technological, cultural, human, as well as political development, discussed as real phenomena. As a result, we are forced into the current usage of these terms, whether we like it or not. Under the circumstances, the least that one can do is make sure that he knows what those terms mean so as to improve communication and understanding. That is precisely what we are trying to do here for the concept of political development.

Definitions are somewhat arbitrary and artificial constructs. It seems that the human mind has a limited capacity to understand and deal with complex phenomena, such as those involving politics and development. Our use of definitions is a way of getting hold of these events by reducing them to simple ideas. This conceptualization of "reality" requires the selection and abstraction of certain facets, while ignoring the rest. For that reason, no definition is complete and can never correspond exactly to the reality it describes.

Through ideal concepts, we try to discern some order in whatever is going on out there. As scientists, we seek patterns and regularities with recurring characteristics which identify and discriminate things at the same time as we relate them to each other. In the attempt to find such characteristics in "political development", we have constructed a conceptual framework to help organize our thoughts. This method, we believe, will clarify things to the reader, as it has to our own mind.

The framework utilizes the well-known elements of systems analysis: structure, function, process, inputs and outputs. We take these elements as the main foci around which to build our case. In order to specify these elements as accurately as possible, we pose the six questions, whose answers usually describe any fact or idea quite reasonably: what? where? who? when? how? why? Accordingly, the conceptual definition of any term should involve six parameters, grouped in three dyads:

1. *Content*: nature or essence of whatever is to be defined;
2. *Context*: structure or arena in which it takes place;
3. *Actors*: units or participants who engage in it;
4. *Action*: factors or conditions accompanying it;
5. *Means*: process or method which it goes through;
6. *Ends*: purpose or function which is served by it.

Together, these six facets describe absolutely anything as completely as possible. On the strength of these answers, we build the multidimensional definition of our subject matter.

Since our subject is political development, we first break down the phrase in its two components and then define each separately. After this analysis, we resynthesize the two and redefine them as a whole. Accordingly the chapter is divided into three sections: Politics; Development; and Political Development. In each one, we go through the same six steps for a comparable definition of politics and development, finally combining the two for the conceptualization of political development. The resulting eighteen items are this product of cross-cutting the three concepts with their six aspects.

Politics

Interactions

To begin with, we conceptualize *politics* by looking at this term as a phenomenon: something which we perceive going on out there. From this point of view, politics is seen as an activity which takes place in reality. Therefore, it appears to be an action or a complex of events happening in what we consider to be the real world.

Politics is a hoary notion and as such has been defined by many people in many ways. In its broadest, politics has been called "the art of the possible" or "the master science". Whether it is an art or a science, politics is a manifold activity that involves a variety of things going on at the same time. As a dynamic and multifaceted phenomenon, politics has been likened to a process of "creative disorder", because it is almost impossible to say what is going on exactly. Nevertheless, it does go on, so people who are fascinated by it try to grapple with its many elusive aspects.

Some of the more significant of these aspects have to do with "power" and "government". From this, more specific, point of view, politics has been defined as "the way to rule people", or "the competition for leadership". Another way of looking at it is to say that politics is a method by which society distributes its values, or "who gets what, when and how". Politics may be all of these things and more; so no single definition does it full justice. All of them focus on one thing that happens to interest whoever does the defining based on little more than subjective and impressionistic opinions; all the way from those that see politics as the "handmaiden of business", to those that look upon it as "the king of the performing arts."

Our approach will be somewhat different. Although one cannot avoid a certain focus and partiality, we try to approach politics from many sides and then strip it of its surface traits to find its essence. All we have said so far is that politics is an *activity*. But, obviously, it is not just any activity. Politics is a particular activity which displays distinctive patterns. At the core of these we can discern some behavioral interaction or transaction in space and time. Let us then begin with this basic notion and elucidate it as we go along.

The Political System

If politics can be seen as a patterned interaction, then it takes place in a network of interrelationships. We cannot conceive of politics in chaos or vacuum, but only within the context of a *system*. This system is not only conceptual but spatial. The total of these relations and activities included in the political system exist in a well-defined area: the *polity* or etymologically the *polis*. In other words, politics is simply what goes on in the polis.

Although, many things were going on in the Greek polis, other than politics, it was politics that was its necessary and sufficient activity. Politics that made the polis more than a society. As we would say now: the political system exists within the social system or society serves as the environment of politics. Of course, the social system need not be a city-state; it could be as small as a family or as large as the world. Politics takes place in many levels and arenas, throughout this broad range from the *micro* to the *macro*.

Whether it is in the agora of the ancient polis or in the United Nations of the modern world, political activity always has a common denominator. It is this underlying trait that distinguishes it from all the other activities going on at the same time in these places. We might say that this distinctive activity is whatever concerns the whole system. No matter what one chooses to define as the system. In this sense, politics is the activity relevant to the things that are common to society: *res publica,* as the Romans said, or "public affairs," as we translate it now.

Politics is whatever is everybody's business in any society; in other words, the opposite of private business, which etymologically is *economics*. This latter was the private affairs of the household and none of the business of the state; whereas politics or *civics*, on the contrary, should precisely interest all the members of the community.

Of course, when we speak of family-politics, we have chosen the family as the relevant system, so politics is whatever interaction pertains to all and is not privy to any particular one. Although politics is a common activity, not all common activities are politics. As we shall see later on, politics is a special kind of public event, which happens under certain conditions and serves certain functions.

Citizenship

So far, we defined politics as a common activity or public affair. This is not sufficient, since we would want to exclude from it circuses and other public spectacles which are not necessarily political. From our etymological perspective, a further delimitation of politics would be made by relating it to its participants As an activity, politics is performed by a group of actors. It takes more than one to play the game; so politics is not a solitary pursuit.

To this quantitative restriction, we must add a qualitative one: the actors in question must be *human beings*. With this postulate, we explicitly limit politics to human societies. Man, as Aristotle said, is *zoon politikon*. Man is the only political animal, although he is not the only social animal.

Ants and bees are social, but apolitical; hence politics can only take place in human societies, and not in anthills or beehives. We cannot conceive of politics going on in other animal societies, though it is very difficult to conceive of any human society in which there is no politics at all. Ideally, one can create a utopia (Plato's *Republic* !?) where politics is excluded by definition, but, precisely for that reason, that society would resemble more a beehive or anthill than any real life human community.

Relatively, some societies are more political than others. We will not go so far as the Greeks to claim that only they were political; but we affirm that by its very nature mankind can only thrive within a polity and not just a society. It is the political *agora* which requires and is defined by the existence of *citizens* as its constituent units. In this case, the citizen is one who partakes of public affairs. Only in this capacity as a participant in political activities is a person a citizen: *polites*. In so far as one does not, he is a private person, *idiotes*; and hence contemptible as an idiot.

This derivation shows quite clearly the high esteem that the ancients had for politics and citizenship. So much so that the only civilized person was the citizen, and politics was synonymous with civilization: *politismos*. Politics, therefore, is a civilized and civilizing activity because it takes place in a *civis* by citizens.

Public Issues

We mentioned that politics is a uniquely human activity because it demands certain peculiarly human attributes. At the center of these attributes is *controversy*. This condition is the *sine qua non* of politics; so we must add "controversial" to the "public human interactions" in the definition of politics. This new qualifier brings us one step closer to the essential conditions for political activity and thus to an understanding of this phenomenon.

By controversy, we mean the existence of differences of opinions, volitions and interests within the social system. That is to say, the existence of "public issues" which characterize "public affairs" in human societies. This trait differentiates human from other social systems. As far as we know, such controversies are to be found only among people and nowhere else. On this ground of controversy politics arises and flourishes.

It is true that *conflicts* do exist among all animals. Such conflicts, however, are articulated as issues only among humans. Here clashes of opinion and contradictions of position surface as verbal rather than physical conflicts. Of course, evolutionary relativity does not allow for clear-cut distinctions among various aspects of animal and human behavior, but we cannot really speak of public issues in anything but a human context.

Be that as it may, politics assumes a *confrontation* of opposing points of view. If there are societies in which everyone is in agreement with everyone else, there cannot be any political activity. Politics abhors harmony. In this sense utopias tend to be apolitical. But, so are dystopias, or any other perfect system.

Although politics thrives on controversy, it requires an underlying consensus provided by a social system. Without it, politics becomes merely physics. Absolutes or extremes of any kind, orderly or chaotic, good or evil, do not allow politics. As Aristotle concluded, only gods are above politics and beasts below it, humans in between are condemned to engage in it.

In this vein, we also conclude that politics is the primordial human or artificial activity, to be found nowhere else on earth, heaven or hell. Politics, thereby, is a civic art or craft that evolved along with culture as a quintessential human activity.

Power Dialectics

Although controversy is a necessary, it is not a sufficient cause of politics. We still have to add another quality pertaining to political activity: the process in which politics handles public issues. Not all human disagreements result in politics; many end up as fights, games or debates. Unlike them, politics is the particular way of dealing with public issues by the judicious manipulation of *power*.

Power has been traditionally tied to politics, yet it is still an ambiguous concept in the social sciences. We do not here attempt another definition of power, but simply borrow that of physics as it tersely equates power (P) to the rate of doing work (W). Since work is done whenever a force (F) accelerates (a) an object (m) some distance (s) over a time (t); the greater the object and the distance, the more work is done and the more power is needed. Hence:

$$P=W/t=Fs/t=mas/t.$$

This physical concept can be translated into politics by replacing the inanimate objects of physics with the human beings of politics. Thus, political power is the capacity to move people; and by that we mean get men to behave in a certain way. The greater the masses one has to move and the further one wants to get them to go in a certain time, the more power one needs. Figuratively speaking, power becomes *influence*, when one tries to make people change their opinions rather than their behavior; when one tries to move minds rather than bodies.

Now, political interactions may be looked upon as an exchange of power or influence: people trying to get each other to think or act in a certain way. But the difference between physics and politics is that the former modifies behavior by the application of physical force, whereas the latter does so by dialectical talk. In politics one does not get physical; the pressure one applies in politics is more subtle, even if it may not always be as effective. Physical force, thus, is antipolitical and whenever it has to be used, we admit political failure.

Rather, the way of politics is a complex play of debate, negotiation, exhortation, bargaining and other non-violent methods, where two opposing sides try to resolve their differences by dialogue.

Form, in politics, then is more important than content: it is not so much what one does but how he does it that defines an act as political. And that "how" must be "civil" or "polite" in the etymological sense, not barbaric which persuades people by other means.

Policy-Making

We complete the definition of politics by adding a final point to those already mentioned. This point relates to the function of politics and directs all political activity towards a particular goal. Politics is a purposive or teleological act. Even if it often is its own reward, politics is undertaken in order to reach some end: public *policy*. The function of politics, therefore, is policy-making.

Politics is supposed to begin in controversy and end in agreement. As such, politics is a way of converting social problems into public policies by means of power dialectics. Of the many ways by which differences may be eliminated, politics provides the one based on *compromise*. It does so, not by eliminating one party in the confrontation but by accommodating both to each other. In politics, there are no complete winners and losers, rights or wrongs, but various degrees of in-betweens. The give and take of politics does not allow for extreme or exclusive solutions; rather, its dialectical method transforms theses and antitheses into an inclusive synthesis.

In systemic terms, the inputs of politics are various opposing pressures transformed through a power algorithm into common outputs. Politics is a process of *conflict-resolution* by collective *decision-making*. Although it is neither the only way of resolving conflicts, nor of making decisions, politics is a particular combination of factors which reconcile contradictions to arrive at a common position. In order to do so, there must be a potential choice and a willingness to make it. In this case, politics provides a procedure of opting among alternatives by calculating the power behind each.

One might say that politics is a *problem-solving* process which uses dialogical, rather than logical or corporal means; so it differs from either mathematics or physics, it is situated somewhere between reason and coercion. Because of that, in its extremes, politics interfaces both *logos* and *chaos* As long as human beings span these two opposing tendencies, politics provide the golden mean for solving their collective problems. Through politics, people are able to orient their collective activities, set their social goals and direct their cultural values with a modicum of civility and common sense.

Development

Directed Change

Development is another complex concept which admits of many interpretations. Moreover, this term has now become heavily weighted with value connotations, so that it can be used to mean just about anything. To avoid these pitfalls, we begin the investigation of "development" by stripping it down to the bare essentials and then adding necessary nuances as we go along.

Apart from its qualitative or subjective aspects, the first thing that development implies is *change*. Whatever else it may mean, development primarily involves some kind of change. In turn, change means a temporal succession of differences within a persisting identity. Change, therefore, combines variation in constancy and as such it pervades "reality".

Within and all around us, we are constantly reminded of this persistence and change. The question whether one or the other prevails is at least as old as Parmenides and Heraclitus, so we will not revive it here. All we can say is that in different historical eras the balance between stability and change shifts from one to the other. It does seem that we now live in one of these periods when the magnitude of change has taken unprecedented proportions. It is for this reason that the topic of social change has become such a fascinating one.

However, development is not just any change but a particular kind. The particularity that characterizes development might be attributed to its *direction*. By adding direction to movement, we get a *vector* quality which can measure both rate and orientation of change.

In the following few pages, we try to discover where that direction leads; keeping in mind that development implies an *evolution* or *anaptixis*; and an unfolding or opening. This etymological meaning can serve as the basic definition which we develop presently.

Meanwhile, we understand development as a purposive or *teleonomic* movement, closely related to the Aristotelian "becoming". As such, developmental change is imbued with some *pattern* or diachronic regularity. It is this pattern that people have sought for a long time, for finding it would give meaning to the past and planning to the future.

Social Systems

Development always happens within a context. Let us postulate the context of development as a *system*. The term is by now sufficiently known not to require a great explanation here. In its simplest form a system is an identifiable aggregate of relations. In more formal terms, it is described as a state vector and a set of connections. If the system is dynamic, the relationships interact, and if the interaction is irreversible, the system changes.

Anything identified as such could be a system: from atomic to cosmic. For our purposes, we could identify two cross-cutting dyads (organic-inorganic and natural-artificial) as the four basic classes of systems which will be discussed here. Different permutations of these give various mixed types, two of which are the *ecosystem* and *sociosystem*. The latter, of particular interest here, is part of the former. The ecosystem forms the environment of the sociosystem, just as the sociosystem is the environment of the political system.

Natural scientists have studied systems much more than social scientists have. If certain analogies hold, the latter stand to learn a lot from the former, particularly in the field of system development. To the natural scientist, development is not such a difficult concept since his teleonomies are rather clear: the acorn develops into an oak and the child into an adult. In all these cases, development involves *growth*, both in quantitative and qualitative terms. The system becomes bigger, more complex and stable, as well as better functioning. In other words, it increases its organization and capability, and by doing so it fulfills its potential.

The question is to what extent can we adopt and adapt the concepts of natural development into social. There is no doubt that all systems have certain isomorphisms; the question is to know whether development is one of them. Fortunately, we do not have to answer this completely in order to proceed with the investigation. So long as we can agree at this point that sociodevelopment could share with ecodevelopment certain points of increasing order and improved efficiency.

Human Growth

In the last section, development was seen from the macrosystemic point of view. Let us now do the same from the micro, which for our purposes is the person. Trying to find some correspondence between human and social development is similar to looking for the analogy between natural and social systems. The question that has often been asked in this context is to what extent should society be considered as "man writ large."

Although this is not the place to engage in this controversy, we make a minimum of assumptions, as in the previous comparison. Humans are natural-cultural beings, therefore their development is largely prescribed in their genetic and environmental givens. Per definition, human development is the road to full maturity of the individual —the actualization of the *human potential*. But apart from the obvious physical characteristics of the fully grown adult, what is the human potential? Is it something that certain people have already attained or is it more of an ideal for the human race. Finally, is that potential fixed and immutable, or does it develop itself in time?

Even if an ideal model for humanity did exist, it is not known for sure; one cannot say what is the final goal of human development, without fear of contradiction. It seems, however, that mankind is always in the process of becoming, so that human needs or wants are ultimately insatiable. It may be that some motive drives mankind to an everlasting search for an elusive fulfillment. Whether one looks upon this process from the point of view of the theory of evolution of humanity throughout the millennia or in the lifetime of a single individual, man is a developing animal: a *homo anaptictus.*

Humans do not develop in isolation. Their social nature requires that even individual development is a collective enterprise. Society provides at least the infrastructure for human development, so it is indispensable to the process. The way social systems persist and change has a direct impact on the form and substance which human development may take. This relationship between the macro and micro contexts indicates that there should be some common elements in the development of both. Whether one considers nature, culture or people, the road to development presents certain parallels which can be elucidated presently.

Energy Potentials

Development can only take place in open, dynamic or living-systems. The reason is that development requires change, and change can only come about if there is some flow of energy. Such flows, in turn, presuppose certain energy differentials between which energy may be upgraded or downgraded. On that assumption, it may be postulated at this point that the development process corresponds to the flow of energy from lower to higher potentials.

Since energy is the capacity to do work, the higher the energy of a system the more capable it is to perform its functions. Open systems draw energy from their environment and then utilize it to maintain their identity and, if possible, grow. Development occurs in the latter phase of a system's attempt to increase its viability. In the process of exchanging matter and energy with its environment, a system will tend to store matter-energy beyond its immediate needs, so as to acquire a margin of safety for is survival. It is this excess which creates the disequilibrium leading to development.

It is the innate drive of all organisms to reach out and affect their environment by assimilating its free matter-energy and reforming it into extension of themselves. This process of development, however, cannot go on indefinitely. The scarcity of available resources and the second law of thermodynamics eventually reverse the development process. Either by reaching maturity or attaining the limits of environmental provisions, a system may maintain a steady-state plateau for a while but, ultimately, will begin to decay and die. Whether by the cycles of their own programs or by the implacable march of *entropy*, all systems gradually break down and disintegrate into the environmental sink.

Development is the struggle against entropy by accumulating a system's ability to control and upgrade energy: creating high potential. By doing so, the system feeds on the environment and, hence, degrades it further. Naturally, everything cannot develop at the same time; the life of some depends on the death of others. All one can do is prolong or extend the process and its effects as far in time and space as possible, thus creating and maintaining islands of energy in a sea of entropy, even if the whole enterprise is doomed in the long run.

Information Syntropy

Part of the energy which systems receive from the environment is in the form of information. As they do with matter-energy in general, systems process information and, thereby, recreate or rearrange it in a multiplicity of new forms and contents. The increased capacity of systems to handle and utilize information in another aspect of development. A system closed to information is autistic and stagnant.

Information is more complex a notion than energy and its many definitions are more abstract. One way of looking at it is to say that information is whatever determines the probability of occurrence for an event. In that sense, it is related to energy which causes events to occur. The greater the relevant information, the more likely it is to determine if something will happen; whereas the greater the available energy, the more possible it is to make it happen. Although some systems may maximize either one or the other, a balanced development would tend to optimize both.

Information, as the term implies, puts things in form or increases pattern and order. Since the very nature of a system is its underlying order, information develops systems. The more complex a system is, the more information it needs to operate, even though it may not need more energy. So, the relation between energy and information is not linear. Although some energy is necessary in order to obtain information, and vice versa; the degradation of energy need not affect information. A system may gain information, while it loses energy.

Nevertheless, the syntropic nature of information should help prolong the overall developmental phase of a system. High information systems are better able to control their activities and manipulate their environment, increasing their viability. Since development is an unstable process, information cannot but help make it more orderly and effective. Without increasing information, development simply becomes physical growth; with information, it becomes *maturity*. Integrated development, means increased control of the homeostasis between the system and its environment, hence maximizing protection from dangerous perturbations. Furthermore, information feedback provides the system with its *learning* capacity, which is the central element in education and development.

Historical Progress

Finally, let us complete the definition of development by mentioning its goals. Why development is the question. From what we have said so far, it would seem that systems develop in order to increase their capacity to respond and perform, so that they become more efficient and effective in their struggle for self-actualization and fulfillment. One could then say that the ontological reason for development is striving for *optimization*.

Naturally, real beings can hardly attain perfection; so what is important is the striving for it. As long as this process shows some returns, development has a meaning and a value. In the realm of human affairs looked upon in historical perspective, this idea of meaningful change for the better is the road to progress. The implication here is of a movement ascending from lower to higher levels of existence.

Whether such vector exists in nature is not known, but it does exist in human ideals. Intelligent or rational systems inevitable produce teleological processes. They formulate and seek a purpose, rather than operate in random or repetitive fashion. In the case of human societies, the purpose of collective development can only be to enhance the individual development of its members. If we accept the humanistic dictum that man is the measure of all things, social development may be justified only in so far as it contributes to human development. This is what is meant when we say that development is the process by which societies become more capable in improving the quality of life of their people.

Apart from the individual striving to satisfy idiosyncratic goals and desires, the human species may be said to have developed throughout history because it can now handle more energy and information than ever before. Human capacity to create and utilize negentropy is higher than any other living system. Of course, what mankind does with this increased ability will determine its ultimate end. Presently, it could destroy itself and the ecosystem, or devise new ways of sustainable development. In any case, human development so far has increased options and choices, thus shifting the responsibility of human destiny from nature to culture.

Political Development
Legitimation

Now that the definitions of "politics" and "development" have been completed separately, they can be combined to form the definition of "political development" (p-d). But since we are here dealing with a vector, rather than a scalar phenomenon, the whole is greater than the sum of its parts. So, we can speak of p-d as the enhanced product of this union.

The first thing that such union requires is the proper identification. Per definition, politics must at some point become explicit and those who engage in it must be aware of what they are doing. Since *consciousness* is a mark of development, until politics is consciously carried out, it cannot be developed. In a state of underdevelopment, politics is haphazard and disoriented. Its activity does not have sufficient regularity and its pattern is not evident. It is only when some pattern can be identified that we become aware of its existence and can say that we know what we are doing.

This evolution from random and nebulous to conscious and defined activity is the first characteristic of p-d. Related to this process is the parallel one of acceptability. As it develops, politics becomes more adapted to its environment and fits in better to the social system, thereby attaining *legitimacy*. When it is underdeveloped, politics either happens spontaneously and sporadically, or it is forcibly imposed and mechanically performed. Otherwise, politics eventually finds its ecological niche and attains sustainable development. It may then be said that p-d is a process of legitimation.

Moreover, p-d acquires of a definite *style* which gives it a certain form and visibility, so that it attains an identity and *integrity* of its own. With p-d, society formulates traditions and codifies the rules of the game; otherwise politics remains anemic, anomic and atrophic. Once it has attained *viability*, one can say that politics has fulfilled the first condition of development. Let us see what this means in the macro and micro levels.

Institutionalization

If politics is public affairs and development is system formation, then p-d must mean the *organizing* process of the polity. In this sense, development applies to the creation and improvisation of the political system: putting public affairs in order. This evolution in general would be the contextual definition of p-d, thus setting the parameters of our subject-matter.

Developing the political system means institutionalizing it: building and promoting political *structures* which can contain political activities within certain bounds. Structure gives action certain identity and visibility; it regularizes and codifies transactions so that they become more predictable and habitual. When political institutions are underdeveloped, politics spills all over the place and yet it is not where it should be. Structure channels and focuses the flow of events, thereby shaping and directing them for particular function. Institutional development tames or modulates politics in order to make it more effective and efficient.

Institutionalization is the backbone of the development of a political *culture*; so a central aspect of cultural development is its increased self-awareness.

This awareness tends to make it more *autonomous* and, therefore, *autarchic*. P-d moves the social system towards greater *self-determination*. As its political institutions become more structured, society is better able to govern itself. Underdeveloped states are rather externally dependent, just as overdeveloped ones extend themselves to dominate others. Between these two extremes, proper p-d provides the optimal sociocybernetic structure.

An important manifestation of this development is the degree of *integration* between the social and political systems. In this sense, "laissez-faire government" would indicate a form of political underdevelopment because of the minimal relations and interactions between the social and political spheres. On the contrary, totalitarianism goes to the other extreme of fusion of the two and, thus, is a type of political overdevelopment. Within these bounds, the structural aspects of p-d indicate the necessary and desirable scope or arena of public affairs within the total system of human activities.

Politicization

As institutionalization is the macro-political manifestation of development, politicization is the micro-political one. From the point of view of the citizens, p-d means the socialization of people into the political system: i.e. citizenship-making. Political socialization develops the political aspects of mankind and brings out the potential of its community spirit. As humans develop, they become political animals to the extent that they fulfill their collective needs.

An apolitical person is a private individual who has no concern for the community. This disinterest shows itself as *apathy* towards public affairs and is usually accompanied by overindulgence in private business. Such extreme individualism or *atomism* in certain societies shows their political underdevelopment; whereas the proper balance between the political, economic and cultural aspects of man indicates an overall social development.

The best index of politicization is the kind and degree of citizen *participation* in public affairs. P-d increases the number of people who participate in politics as well as it increases their depth of commitment. Wider citizen involvement makes the political system grow at least quantitatively by making it more inclusive. On the contrary, political *elitism* or exclusivity indicates political underdevelopment. In these cases, *alienation* characterizes the average person who cannot participate in social life. Isolating people from the agora privatizes them and undermines p-d.

At the other extreme, hyperpoliticization would raise the activity of people to heights of paroxysm. A feverish political action cannot be maintained for long without explosive consequences. Politics, like many other activities, become dangerous when overdone because they raise expectations which cannot be fulfilled. When people become super-political, they end up monomanic: unidimensional persons obsessed with a single aspect of existence, while ignoring all the others. Fanatics, like idiots, do not make good citizens; so a political system with too many of either extreme cannot be too developed. Rather, a "happy versatility" and *pas trop de zèle* seem to be just the right ingredients for p-d.

Mobilization

From what has been said so far, the factors which make for p-d are multiple and variable. Since public issues are the conditions for politics and energy differentials are the conditions for development, then p-d would require some combination of these inputs to converge at the same time and place. This means that there must arise differences of interest and opinion coupled with differences of energy and potential. The interaction of these *differentials* then is the necessary, but not sufficient, cause of p-d.

Political systems effect social change when the pressures or demands made upon them cannot be handled by established routines. The triggering of p-d, therefore, begins with increasing *challenges* to the system. A developing polity exhibits great dynamism and a high level of activity because its inputs are increasing. To put it another way, if one wants p-d, he begins by the *mobilization* of various forces for change. This new energy input must be sufficient to overcome the inertia of the system and push it to a higher state of action. In these circumstances, political *agitation* may break the passivity of the system and get it to move ahead.

However, politics is a dangerous activity. It is time and energy intensive, thus highly entropic. Politics burns a lot of human energy; it enervates its actors and tends to exhaust the environment. Intensive political activity generates a lot of heat, which if not quickly absorbed or dissipated, can end up a horrible conflagration. An underdeveloped political system cannot handle sudden jumps of such energy without short-circuiting. Sustained p-d must proceed prudently by a gradual progression in the stimulus-response spiral.

A developed political system should be able to absorb and process great amounts of public energy; so much so that it would welcome and thrive on challenging issues. For that reason, it must have good enough sensors to *anticipate* and machinery to *prepare* for these eventualities. In this way it could face crises without panic reactions which lead to extreme behavior. P-d leads to greater *self-control* and measured response to environmental challenges. Although social change can be brought about without p-d, it is only through p-d that it could be assured of moderation and regulation. As we see in the next section, these characteristics of p-d require an increased capacitation of the political system.

Capacitation

A crucial question of p-d is how to increase the capacity of the system to handle heavier loads. P-d cannot begin until the machinery of the system shows some inadequacies in operating under new conditions. In this case, if the heavy pressures do not subside and if the machine does not break down, p-d would improve the performance of the system and make it equal to the challenge.

The political process, it is already agreed, utilizes power to influence human behavior. This operation unavoidably expends energy and, hence, increases the entropy of the system or of the environment. On the other hand, development is a syntropic process because it increases information and organization.

By combining these two complementary tendencies, p-d can prevent the excesses of hyperpoliticization and maldevelopment. The agonistic spirit of man may be tempered through education and political action may be kept within bounds by an enlightened body politic. As the Greeks understood a long time ago, politics requires a certain level of social development, including leisure and learning *(scholé* and *paidea)*.

In this sense, p-d means balancing as well as increasing the levels of energy and information in the system. Great asymmetries between the two may bring about other kinds of social change but not p-d. High levels of energy interactions require knowledgeable and careful operators. Increased political activity necessitates a highly sophisticated and self-restrained citizenry. Wielding great power takes talent and *prudence* which only wise and *responsible* people can handle.

This process of political *enlightenment* involves improving methods for collective articulation and deliberation, cooperation and coordination, as well as diplomacy and democracy. To develop such formidable capacities, the polity must plan and rationalize its operations. As a system becomes more complex, it becomes more vulnerable; so it has to increase its tolerance to disturbances: both internal and external. It must prepare not only more flexible responses but more creative initiatives. In other words, p-d contributes the improved problem-solving capability and increased policy-making efficiency of the social system.

Civilization

Finally, we complete the definition of p-d by considering its function. Using our conceptual framework, this function is a combination of the political and developmental processes leading to policy-progress.

This means that the output of p-d should be improved collective decision-making for the fulfillment of human aspirations. The development of public policy serves the common attainment of social and personal ends.

Although p-d is good in itself because it fulfills one aspect of human nature, it also promotes other human goals. P-d makes it possible for all those who are affected by public affairs to take part in shaping public policy. This enhanced opportunity to participate in decision-making makes p-d an instrumental *human-right*. Since those who participate in the making of policies are more likely to respect and implement them, involvement in public affairs tends to civilize men.

P-d makes people more sociable and empathetic, more communicative and understanding, as well as more critical and eclectic. Political maturity means easier acceptance of conflicts and contradictions, the ability to live with uncertainty and insecurity. P-d imposes self-limitations to one's claims and expectations; it serves as an internal control of one's wants. It is an understanding that everybody cannot have everything at the same time and that social life demands consideration of others. In this sense, p-d contributes to *moral* development by promoting the accommodation of conflicting interests.

Both political immaturity and immorality manifest themselves in egoistic expectations, without taking into account the needs and wishes of others. Such underdevelopment leads to brutality and terrorism. On the contrary, p-d balances one's private interests with the common good, by promoting concern and commitment without fanaticism or nihilism.

P-d will by no means solve all the problems of the human condition. Politics is no panacea for every social ill. In many cases it may exacerbate and worsen things. But, whatever the outcome, p-d will bring it about through *consensus*, thereby making people responsible by attributing to them full credit or blame for their decisions.

Having completed the defining elaborations, we are ready to summarize what has been said in more concise terms. The following, then, serves as the composite definitions of the three terms:

— *Politics* is citizen interaction in public affairs, trying to resolve conflicting issues by power dialectics, resulting in collective policies.
— *Development* is directed change, actualizing system potential by increasing energy and information capability, aiming to satisfy set values.
— *Political Development* is a process of legitimation and institutionalization of public affairs by politicization and mobilization, thus improving system capacity to attain social objectives.

Attempting to arrive at a precise definition of complex concepts is a convoluted affair. One is forced to opt for either rigor or clarity, but the correspondence between concept and reality always leaves something to be desired. As a result, we tried to arrive at an optimal position which gives maximum understanding with minimum distortion.

As a further aid to clarification, we constructed a *synoptic* table which contains all the key terms which we underlined in the course of this essay. The tabulation of these terms in the following page should give an overall idea of the various elements which have gone into the definitions, along with their interrelationships. This will supplement the above definitions by adding certain nuances to the terms used therein.

Synoptic Matrix

TOPIC / PHASE	I POLITICS	II DEVELOPMENT	III P-D
POWER			
1 NATURE FORM CONTENT	INTERACTION Phenomenon Activity Event	DIRECTION Evolution Vector Anaptixis	LEGITIMATION Identity Integrity Viability
2 ARENA STRUCTURE CONTEXT	POLITY Res Publica Civics Public	SOCIETY Growth Potential Environment	INSTITUTION Organization Integration Autonomy
3 ACTORS ROLES ELEMENTS	CITIZENSHIP Zoon Politikon Polites Urbality	MATURATION Homo Anaptictus Actualization Realization	POLITICIZATION Participation Involvement Empathy
4 INPUTS FACTORS CONDITIONS	ISSUES Controversy Conflict Controntation	ENERGY Dynamism Imbalance Entropy	MOBILIZATION Challenge Anticipation Control
5 PROCESS METHOD CONVERSION	POWER Dialectics Influence Work	INFORMATION Syntropy Knowledge Order	CAPACITATION Leisure Education Prudence
6 OUTPUTS GOALS FUNCTIONS	POLICY Compromise Resolution Accomodation	PROGRESS Improvement Meaning History	CIVILIZATION Rights Morality Consensus

Moreover, the table also serves to illustrate the entire conceptual framework of the chapter. In effect, the table is the *matrix* resulting by interposing the three subjects of the definition with the method used in defining them. The horizontal gives the three sections of this chapter, and the vertical, the six items of each. Another elucidation is provided in the table by grouping the vertical sections into the top three representing the main system parameters (form-structure-actors) and the bottom three representing the system process (input-conversion-output). With these preliminaries, the table contents should be self-explanatory.

We conclude with some suggestions for the logical follow-up of this work. The definition of terms is the first step in understanding concepts, so what was done here is the prolegomenon to any systematic research into a subject. An attempt at conceptualization must precede any in-depth study of a topic, so that the investigator knows what is to be done.

Having done that, the next step is to put the definition to work. This means converting the conceptual into an *operational* definition. To do so, one has to find empirical *indices* for the various elements of the definition. These indicators should be as observable and measurable as possible, so that they can test the correspondence between the concepts and reality. In this case, operationalization should not be that difficult, but testing the indicators would present many problems because of the penury of comparative political statistics.

Be that as it may, another phase of scientific study is the formulation and testing of *hypotheses*. Once concepts have been defined, one tries to find relevant correlations among them. In this case, an interesting study would try to discern any links between political and economic development. Similarly, one could investigate the relation between political development and a host of other phenomena of particular significance to the researcher.

These and other possible studies should enhance our knowledge of political development and the place it occupies in human lives. This increased knowledge will provide the necessary feedback to improve our conceptualization of reality and, thereby, ameliorate human capacity to set and attain collective goals. Although politics may not be the most important thing in human affairs, p-d would definitely contribute both to the means and ends or processes and policies of social progress. Further research in this area should, therefore, be essential to our common enterprise.

Conclusion

This book began by discussing the global problematique, then engaged in an analytic situation study of certain critical aspects of the contemporary world and ended by proposing various courses of action contributing to its resolution.

The general hypothesis throughout was that the main culprit for the present problems is massive and uncontrolled industrialization, initiated by the countries of the North-Western World. On this basis, it is our thesis that the solution for the foreseeable future has to be found in the policies of the so-called First World countries which are now in full transition to the postmodern era. Their economic, political, and cultural similarities put them in a privileged position at the vanguard of history; therefore the direction they take from here will determine the fate of all mankind.

For this reason, this study has carried out a social *diagnosis, anagnosis,* and *prognosis* of the human condition and concluded with a recommended *therapy* which can make the transition less painful and the result more healthful.

This means that the work was undertaken with three explicit foci:

1. *Problem-solving*: effective political resolution of actual public issues;
2. *Forward-planning*: timely proaction on emerging global problems;
3. *Policy-making*: consensual definition of desired social objectives.

It is this trio that makes up the politics of postmodernism and characterizes the decision-making process of prototechnologic societies. It is these advanced systems which are now in the best position to deal with the problems they have created and lead the whole world to better conditions.

Having said that, however, one must not forget that neat synthetic packages such as the one drawn here are ideal models which only approximate reality. Human beings and their societies are rather messy and largely unpredictable, so nothing can be said with certainty about them. Behavior and evolution, of which political development is a part, result from a combination of deterministic and chaotic, as well as intentional factors. Human ideas and wants count only partially in this historical causality which leaves various eventualities open to random fluctuations.

With this caveat of humility, as well as a combination of the Theory of Sociophysics and the method of general systems, it is possible to correlate human society with both its natural context and political content. In particular, these relations apply to the structures and functions of the post-modern system as it interacts with its external environments and its internal constituents.

The conceptual framework chosen to analyze these interfaces is a three-dimensional construct involving spatial, temporal, and thematic aspects. In the first place, the *geographical* context included the local, national, and global levels of aggregation. The centrality of the nation-state in this scheme focused the discussion at the middle layer, with relevant excursions at both higher and lower levels.

Next, the unidimensionally of the *historical* context divided the discussion into past, present and future periods. These fall chronologically into the traditional agricultural, modern industrial, and post-modern technological waves of macrohistory. In this sequence, the most advanced societies of the First World are now undergoing the transformation between industrial and postindustrial development.

Finally, the *thematic* content consists of the primary factors responsible for this transformation of the main elements composing postmodern societies. We isolated these as the scientific advances and technological innovations which brought about the well-known revolutionary changes in human society, economy, and polity. The dynamic interdependence among these five variables then served as the *cyberpolitical* SPECT model and set the agenda for our subsequent discussion. Applied to the specifications of the *infosociety,* these variables were separated into the politic and informatic subsystems which intersected each other in the transmission of influence and data. In that case, the flow of social information also triggers the exchange of political influence: hence, the phenomenon of *infopolitics.*

This systemic aspect of postmodernism was then juxtaposed with its environmental aspects by considering the interface between culture and nature. From this point of view, *ecopolitics* tries to resolve the public issues arising from the movement to convert consumer into conserver societies. This can best be done by taking advantage of infotechnology which allows a more legitimate process of *gaiapolitics* throughout the world, taking into account not only the interests of more people but also of the entire *ecosystem.*

Focusing on democracy as the central concern of postmodernism, we then demonstrated how a *technosociety* could avoid being a technocracy. By utilizing its network of telecommunications, a postmodern community can become a Teledemocracy. The high-tech structures of postindustrial systems thus make possible a wider and easier participation in public affairs. In this case, the advancement of political science and technology can lead to the art and craft of *technopolitics,* by applying the new ways and means to involve more people in collective policy-making. Finally, this process was defined as political development in the essay on *metapolitics.*

The proper synthesis of all these aspects is the essence of *sociopolitics.* which results from an increasing concern for sustainable development. As people become more enlightened and sophisticated, they also behave more sociopolitically. That is to say, they try to resolve their conflicts by dialectical means, so as to optimize the common interest. Therefore, political development leads to the morality of sociopolitics which is, after all, the highest stage of human civilization.

Analytic Index

CHAPTER ONE
Cyberpolitics
Science, Technology and Society

I - DEFINITIONS

1. Introduction: Problem and Purpose; Form and Content
2. System: Theory and Method; Society and Nature (Matrix of Components)

II - FOCI

3. Actions: Functional Activities, Five Main Roles
4. Actors: Behavioral Groups, Five Institutional Types (Spect Model)

III - LOCI

5. Relations: Intergroup Connections, Thirty Bilateral Ties (System Network)
6. Interactions: Channel Flows, Three Types of Activity (Input-Output Table)

IV - ACTA

7. Progress: Chronological Sequence, Operative Cycle (Flow Chart)
8. Conclusion: Summary and Overview, Research Agenda

CHAPTER TWO
Infopolitics
Political Power in Infosocieties

I - POLITICS AND INFORMATICS

1. The Political System
2. The Informatic System
   (Politics-Informatics Interface Model)
3. The Info-Politics Model
4. *Scientia Potestas Est*
5. Infopolitical Power

II - TECHNOLOGICAL TRENDS AND IMPACTS

1. Technological Revolution and Information Society
2. Informatic Technology and Political Change
3. The Technocratic Scenario
4. The Democratic Scenario
5. Technics and Politics

III - GEOPOLITICS OF INFORMATIC ECONOMY

1. Informatic Technology and Political Geography
2. Localization of Informatics and Micropolitics
3. National Politics and Informatic Systems
4. Nations in the International System
5. Geography and Technology

IV - POLICY-MAKING IN INFOSOCIETY

1. Informational and Political Technology
   (The Information-Policy Process)
2. Policy-Identification
3. Policy-Intention
4. Policy-Implementation
5. Political Technology

CHAPTER THREE
Ecopolitics
Societies in the Postindustrial Era

I - EVOLVING CONDITIONS
Contributive factors for the Consumer Society

A. ECONOMIC INFRASTRUCTURE
Technical Innovation; Industrial Growth; Market System; Consumer Society

B. SOCIAL REPERCUSSIONS
Conserver Debate; Distributive Justice; Political Equality; Human Crisis

C. POLITICAL PARTICIPATION
Socialization; Decentralization; Coordination; Legitimation

II - ALTERNATIVES
Social Transformation Policies

A. PREPARATORY ACTIVITIES
Political Expediency; Social Planning; State Priorities; Social Change

B. POLICY ALTERNATIVES
Traits; Production-Control;Consumption-Regulation; Distribution-Equity

C. POLITICAL ACTION
Conflict; Resistance; Participation; Initiative

III - THE OPTIMAL ECOSOCIETY
Preferable Future Scenario

A. POLITICAL CULTURE
Value-Orientation; Social Health; Permanent Education; Steady-State

B. SOCIO-ECONOMIC STRUCTURE
Work and Leisure; Activity and Welfare; Private Property; Public Sector

C. PUBLIC INSTITUTIONS
Technology Assessment; Communication; Organization; Ecopolicy Options

295

CHAPTER FOUR
Gaiapolitics
The Ecosociety in a Turbulent World

IV - PARAMETERS
Environmental Inputs from the World System

A. TRANSNATIONAL INTERDEPENDENCE
Modernization; TNC's; Global Integration; Ecosystem Entropy

B. GEOPOLITICAL CONFLICTS
East-West; North-South; Industrial Development; Interest Coalitions

C. NATION-STATE SOVEREIGNTY
Nationalism; Internationalism; Intranationalism; Separatism

V - ALTERNATIVES
Foreign Policy Options

A. ETHNOCENTRIC NATIONALISM
Foreign Policy; National Interest; Isolationism; Economic Nationalism

B. NORTHERN REGIONALISM
Supra-Nationalism; European; North American; Third World

C. GLOBAL INTERNATIONALISM
Multilateralism; Policy Priorities; Foreign Aid; Activist Diplomacy

VI - THE GLOBAL SYSTEM
A Global Ecosociety

A. EARTH POLITICS
Scenarios; Redistribution; Political Development; Conflict-Cooperation

B. WORLD ORGANIZATION
Internationalization; Organization; Institutionalization; Conservation

C. UNIVERSAL VALUES
Cosmic Ideology; Human Values; Cosmopolitan Morality; Policy Principles

CHAPTER FIVE
Technopolitics
Telecommunitary Democracy

First Part: Structures

I - CONCEPTS
Scope & Content

1 - Political Development
2 - Information Society
3 - Telecommunitary Democracy

II - ACTORS
Groups & Individuals

1 - Politicians & Administrators
2 - Citizens & Lobbies
3 - Experts & Mediators

III - ARENAS
Levels of Action

1 - Local - Community
2 - Nation - State
3 - Global - World

Analytic Index

Second Part: Functions

IV - INPUTS
Environmental Factors

1 - Human Needs
2 - Social Demands
3 - Policy Plans

V - CONVERSIONS
Political Interactions

1 - Confrontation of Issues
2 - Negotiation of Positions
3 - Accommodation of Interests

VI - OUTPUTS
Policy Results

1 - Decision-Taking
2 - Executive Implementation
3 - Feedback Evaluation

CHAPTER SIX
Metapolitics
Political Development

CONTENT TABULATION

I. POLITICS   II. DEVELOPMENT   III. POL-DEV.

1. Interactions	Directed Change	Legitimation
2. Political System	Social Systems	Institutionalization
3. Citizenship	Human Growth	Politicization
4. Public Issues	Energy Potentials	Mobilization
5. Power Dialectics	Info Syntropy	Capacitation
6. Policy-making	Historical Progress	Civilization

Thematic Bibliography

The academic trappings of this book have been kept to the minimum. The many (over 400) sources used have not been directly quoted or footnoted in the text because the ideas contained therein are not exclusive to any author but are shared by different ones in various degrees. For that reason, direct attribution would have resulted in multiple and repetitive citations which would have unnecessarily burdened the arguments without changing the spirit of the conclusions.

The following bibliography lists only the main authorities on whom this essay is based. The breakdown follows the thematic organization as it is outlined in the table of contents. Again, to avoid repetition, each source has been cited only once in the section where its main contribution lies; even though it may also support the arguments in other sections.

Infosociety

Science

Arnopoulos, P.J. (ed.) *S & T Policy Documents*. Gamma-Concordia, Mtl, 1981.

Blume, S. *Towards a Political Sociology of Science*. Free Press, N.Y., 1977.

Behrman, D. *S & T In Development*. UNESCO, Paris, 1977.

Boulloche, A. et.al. *Science et Democratie* Futuribles, Paris, 1977.

Chaszer, E. *S & T in Social & Political Alienation*. George Washington U, 1969

Fusfeld, H.I. (ed.) *S & T Policy:* New York Academy of Sciences, N.Y., 1979.

Greenberg, D.S. *The Politics of Pure Science*. N.A.L., N.Y., 1968.

Haas, E.B. *Scientists & World Order*. University of California, Berkeley, 1977

Hiskes, A.L.D. *Science, Technology & Policy*. Westview, Boulder, 1986

Hoffman, L.M. *The Politics of Knowledge*. SUNY, Albany, 1989

Huddle, F. & W. Johnston. *S-T & Diplomacy*. Library of Congress, Wash, 1976.

Jackson, R.W. *Human Goals & Science Policy*. Science Council, Ottawa, 1976.

Jones, H.W. *Law and the Social Role of Science*. Rockefeller, N.Y., 1966.

Ladriere, J. *The Cultural Challenge of S & T*. UNESCO, Paris, 1977.

Lakoff, S.A. (ed.) *Knowledge and Power*. Free Press, N.Y., 1966.

Langley, P. *et.al. Scientific Discovery*. The MIT Press, Cambridge, 1987

Moraze, C. *Science and the Factors of Inequality*. UNESCO, Paris, 1979.

National Academy of Sciences. *Science & Technology*. Freeman, S.F., 1979.

Nelson, W.R. (ed.) *The Politics of Science*. Oxford, N.Y., 1968.

Oettinger, Bearman, Read. *High & Low Politics*. Pallinger, Cambridge, 1977.

Patterson, E. *Law in a Scientific Age*. Columbia, N.Y., 1963.

Price, D.K. *The Scientific Estate*. Harvard, Cambridge, 1965.

Ruberti, A. (Ed) *System Science & Modelling*. Reidel/Unesco, Paris. 1984

Sackman, H. *Computers, Systems Science & Evolving Society*. Wiley, N.Y., 67.

Schwartz, E.S. *Overskill*. Ballantine, N.Y., 1971.

Sheinin, Y. *Science Policy*. Progress Publishers, Moscow, 1978.

Policy

Allison, D. *Decision-Making in a Changing World*. Innovation, Princeton, 1971.

Arnopoulos,P.J. (Ed). *Public Policy Papers*. Concordia, Montreal, 1992

Eyestone, R. *From Social Issues to Public Policy*. Wiley, N.Y., 1978.

Forester, J. *Planning in the Face of Power*. California U.P. Berkeley, 1989

Kaplan, N. et.al.*Social Knowledge & Policy Decisions*. Michigan, Ann Arbor, 75

Lindblum, C.A. and D.K. Cohen. *Usable Knowledge*. Yale, N.Y., 1979.

Mayer, R. & E. Greenwood. *Design of Social Policy Research*. P-H, N.J., 1980.

Mowitz, R.J. *Design of Public Decision Systems*. University Park, Balt, 1980.

Nagel, S.S. *Global Policy Studies*. Macmillan, Basingstobe, 1991

Navarro, P. *The Policy Game*. Wiley, N.Y. 1984

Nelkin, D. *The Politics of Technical Decisions*. Sage, London, 1979.

Rein, M. *Social Science and Public Policy*. Penguin, Middlesex, 1976.

Sewell, W. & J. Coppock (eds.) *Public Participation Planning*. Wiley, London, 77.

Sharkanski, J. (ed.) *Policy Analysis in Political Science*. Markham, Chicago, 70

Tugwell, F. *Search for Alternatives.*, Winthrop, Cambridge, 1973.

Weiss, C.H. (eds.) *Social Research & Public Policy-Making*. Lexington, 1977.

Wilenski, H.L. *Organizational Intelligence*. Basic Books, N.Y., 1967.

Zaltman, G. and R. Duncan. *Strategy for Planned Change*. Wiley, N.Y., 1977.

Cybernetics

Arnopoulos, P.J. "Ideal-Real Links." *Kybernetes*, Manchester, 1993

Benveniste, G. *The Politics of Expertise*. Glendessary, Berkely, 1972.

Bell, D.V.J. *Resistance and Revolution*. Houghton-Mifflin, Boston, 1973.

Dechert, C.R. (ed.) *The Social Impact of Cybernetics*. Notre Dame, 1966.

Ellul, J. *Propaganda*. Knopf, N.Y., 1967.

Finlay, M. *Powermatics*. Routledge & Kegan Paul, N.Y. 1990

Kennedy, M.M. *Powerbase*. Macmillan, N.Y. 1984

Lackey, S. *Strategy for a Living Revolution*. Freeman, San Francisco, 1973.

McBride, R. *The Automated State*. Chilton, N.Y., 1967.

Mumford, L. *The Pentagon of Power*. Harcourt-Brace, N.Y., 1970.

Ricci, E.J. *Cybernetics and Society*. Miter, Washington, 1969.

Rule, J. *Private Lives and Public Surveillance*. Albert Lane, London, 1976.

Shepard, J.M. *Automation and Alienation*. MIT, Cambridge, 1971.

Simmie, J. *The State in Action*. Pinter, London, 1990

Suttles, G. & Zald, M. (Eds). *Challenge of Social Control*. Ablex, Norwood, 1985

Tufte, E.R. *Political Control of the Economy*. Princeton, N.Y., 1978.

Informatics

Anderla, G. *Information in 1985*. OECD, Paris, 1973.

Bagdinian, B. *Information Machines & Their Impact*. Harper & Row, N.Y, 1971

Development Dialogue. *A New World Information & Communication Order*. Dag Hammarskjold Foundation, Uppsala, Sweden, 1981.

Ekecrantz, J. et.al. *The Politics of Information*. Amsterdam U Press, 1976.

Hammer, D.P. *The Information Age*. Scarecrow Press, N.J., 1976.

Hellman, J. *Privacy and Information Systems*. Rand, S.B., 1980.

Lempen, B. *Information et Pouvoir*. L'Age d'Homme, Lausanne, 1980.

Masuda, Y. *The Information Society*. World Future Society, Washington, 1981.

MacBride, Sean, et.al. *Many Voices, One World*. UNESCO, Paris, 1980.

McHale, J. *The Changing Information Environment*. Paul Elek, 1976.

Nora, S. & A. Mink. *L'Informatisation de la Société*. Doc Française, Paris, 1978.

Oyama, S. *The Ontogeny of Information*. Cambridge U.P. 1985

Penzias, A. *Ideas & Information*. Touchstone, N.Y. 1989

Poppel, H. & Goldstein, B. *Information Technology*. McGraw-Hill, N.Y. 1987

Porat, M.V. *The Information Economy*. U.S. Government, Washington, 1977.

Ranney, A. *Channels of Power*. Basic Books, N.Y. 1983

Sackman, H. & N. Nie (eds.) *Information Utility & Social Change*. Afips, N.J., 70.

Servan-Schreiber, J-L. *The Power to Inform*. McGraw-Hill, N.Y., 1974

U.S. Government. *Advanced Information Technology*. Washington, 1973.

Westin, A.F. *Information Technology in a Democracy*. Harvard, Cambridge, '71

Computers

Diebold, J. *Man, the Computer & Technology* Praeger, N.Y., 1969

Dickson, P. *The Electronic Battlefield*. Indiana U., Bloomington, 1977.

Eaton, J. *Computers and Socialism*. Spokesman Press, Nottingham, 1973.

Gotlieb, C. & A. Borodin. *Social Issues in Computing*. Academic Press, 1973.

Hawkes, N. *The Computer Revolution*. Thames and Hudson, London, 1971.

James, M. *The Computerized Society*. Prentice-Hall, N.Y., 1970.

Johnson, D.W. *Computer Ethics*. Brethren Press, Elgin, 1984

Kraemer, K.L. *Computers and local Government*. Praeger, N.Y., 1977.

Landon, K.C. *Computers and Bureaucratic Reform*. Wiley, N.Y., 1974.

Laver, M. *Computers and Social Change*. Cambridge U. Press, London, 1980.

Laurie, E.J. *Computers, Automation & Society*. R.D. Irwin, Homewood, 1979.

Martin, J. & A. Norman. *The Computerized Society*. Prentice-Hall, N.J., 1970.

Montague, A. & S. Snyder. *Man & the Computer*. Auerbach, Philadelphia, 1972.

Mumford, E. *Computers: Planning for People*. Batsford, London, 1968.

Mumford, E. & H. Sackman. *Human Choice in Computers*. North Holland, 1975.

Nora, S. & A. Minck. *The Computerization of Society*. MIT, Cambridge, 1980.

Pagels, H.R. (Ed) *Computer Culture*. New York Academy of Sciences. 1987

Pool, I et al *Communications, Computers & Automation* UNITAR, N.Y., 1971.

Pylyshyn, Z.W.*Perspectives on the Computer Revolution*. Prentice Hall, N.J.'70.

Remer, R.W. (ed.) *Computers and Crisis*. A.C.M., N.Y., 1971.

Taviss, J. *The Computer Impact*. Prentice Hall, N.Y., 1970.

Teague, R. & C. Erickson. *Computers and Society*. West Pub., St. Paul, 1974.

Wessel, R. *The Computer's Threat to Society*. Addison-Wesleyu, 1974.

Ecosociety

Ecology

Bradbury, J.K. *The Biosphere*. Belhaven, N.y. 1991

Brown, L.R. *The State of the World*. Norton, N.Y. 1991

Cairncross, F. *Costing the Earth*. Harvard, Cambridge, 1992

Cole, H.S.D. et.al (eds.) *Models of Doom* Universe Books, N.Y. 1975.

Eckersley, R. *Environmentalism & Political Theory*. SUNY, N.Y. 1991

Fleming, D.F. *The Issues of Survival*. Doubleday, N.Y., 1973

Forrester, J.W. *World Dynamics*. Wright-Allen, Cambridge, 1971.

Fuller, Buckminster, R. *Earth Inc*. Doubleday, N.Y., 1973.

Falk, R. *This Endangered Planet*. Vintage Books, N.Y., 1972.

Goldsmith, M. (ed.) *The Predicament of Man*. In-for-link, London, 1972.

Galtung, J. *The True Worlds*. North-Holland, Amsterdam, 1975.

Harte, J. & R. Soclow, *The Patient Earth*. Holt-Rinehart-Winston, N.Y, 1971

Hamilton, M. (ed.) *This Little Planet*. Scribners, N.Y., 1970.

Heilbroner, R.L. *The Human Prospect*. Norton, N.Y., 1974.

Joseph, L.E. *Gaia*. St. Martin's, N.Y. 1990

Land, S.T.L. *Grow or Die*. Random-House, N.Y. 1973

Laszlo, E. (ed.) *The World System*. Braziller, N.Y., 1973.

Mendlovitz, S.H. (ed.) *The Creation of a Just World Order*. Free Press, N.Y,1975

Meadows, D. et.al. *The Limits to Growth*. New American Library, N.Y., 1972.

Mesarovic, M & E. Pestel. *Mankind at the Turning Point*. Dutton, N.Y., 1974.

Mitchell, J.G. *Ecotactics*. Pocket Books, N.Y. 1970

Moskowitz, M. *The Global Marketplace*. Macmillan, N.Y. 1988

Muroyama, J. & Stever, G. (Eds). *Globalization of Technology*. NAP, Wash.1988

Ohmae, K. *Triad Power*. Free Press, N.Y. 1985

Radest, H.B. *To Seek A Humane World*. Pemberton, London, 1971.

Rifkin, J. *Biosphere Politics*. Crown, N.Y. 1991

Sprout, H. & M. *Towards a Politics of the Planet Earth*. Nostrand, N.Y., 1971.

Slater, P. *Earth Walk*. Anchor/Doubleday, N.Y., 1974.

Schumacher, E.F. *Small is Beautiful*. Harper-Torchbooks, N.Y., 1973.

Smith, R.L. (ed.) *The Ecology of Man*. Harper & Row, N.Y. 1972.

Sutter, K. *Reshaping the Global Agenda*. UNA, Sydney, Australia, 1986

Swift, A. *Global Political Ecology*. Pluto, London, 1993

Toffler, A. *Future Shock*. Random House, N.Y., 1970.

Tosches, N. *Power on Earth*. Random House, N.Y. 1986

Wagar, W. *Building the City of Man*. Freeman, S. F, 1971.

Ward, B. *Spaceship Earth*. Columbia University, N.Y., 1966.

Weisberg, B. *Beyond Repair: The Ecology of Capitalism*. Beacon, Boston, 1971

Futurology

Arnopoulos, P.J. *Mediterranean 2000*. I.M.S. Athens, 1992

Barron, J. and R. Curnnow. *The Future of Microelectronics*. Nickols, 1979.

Bell, W. & J. Ma (eds.) *The Sociology of the Future*. Russell Sage, N.Y., 1971.

Beres, L.R. & H.R. Targ. *Planning Alternative World Futures*. Praeger, N.Y. 1975.

Brzezinski, Z. *Between Two Ages*. Viking, N.Y., 1970.

Celente, G. *Trend Tracking*. Wiley, N.Y. 1990

Davis, S.M. *Future Perfect*. Addison-Wesley, Reading, 1987

Dordick, H.S. et.al. *The Emerging Network Marketplace*. Ablex, N.J., 1980.

Dublin, M. *Futurehype*. Penguin, Markham, 1989

Falk, R. *A Study of Future Worlds*. The Free Press, N.Y., 1975.

Feather, F. (ed.) *Through the Eighties*. W.F.S., Washington, 1980.

Forester, T. (ed.) *The Microelectronic Revolution*. Blackwell, Toronto, 1980.

Ferrarotti, F. *Five Scenarios for the Year 2000*. Greenwood, N.Y. 1986

Foster, H. *Postmodern Culture*. Pluto Press, London, 1985

Giarini, O. *The Emerging Service Economy*. Pergamon, Oxford, 1987

Grunig, J. *The Decline of the Global Village*. General Hall, N.Y., 1976.

Hill, C. & J. Ufferback (eds.) *Technological Innovation*. Pergammon, N.Y., 1979.

Hirsch, F. *Social Limits to Growth*. Harvard, Cambridge, 1976.

Hostrop, R.W. (ed.) *Foundations of Futurology* E.T.C., Homewood, 1973.

Kettle, J. *Footnotes on the Future*. Methuen, Toronto, 1970.

Lindberg, L.N. (ed.) *Politics & the Future of Industrial Society*. McKay, N.Y., 76.

Miller, S. and P. Roby. *The Future of Inequality*. Basic Books, N.Y., 1970.

Muller, H.J. *Uses of the Future*. Indiana U. Press, Bloomington, 1974.

National Research Council. *Outlook for S & T*. Freeman, S.F., 1982.

Ong, W.J. (ed.) *Knowledge and the Future of Man*. Simon & Shuster, N.Y, 1968

Platt, J. *Perception and Change*. U. of Michigan, Ann Arbor, 1970.

Roslanski, J.D. (ed.) *Shaping the Future*. North Holland, Amsterdam, 1972.

Somit, A. *Political Science & the Study of the Future*. Dryden, Hinsdale, '74.

Strong, M.F. *Alternative Courses for the Human Future*. C.I.I.A. Toronto, 1974.

Toynbee, A. *Surviving the Future*. Oxford University Press, London, 1971.

Teich, A.H. (ed.) *Technology & Man's Future*. St. Martin's, N.Y., 1977.

Toffler, A. *Power/Shift*. Bantham, N.Y. 1990

Vacca, R. *The Coming Dark Age*. Doubleday Anchor, N.Y., 1974.

Weiner, J. *The Next Hundred Years*. Bantam, N.Y. 1990

Wallia, C.S. (ed.) *Towards Century 21*. Basic Books, N.Y., 1970.

Sociology

Arnopoulos, P.J. *Sociophysics*. Nova Science Publishers, N.Y. 1993

Bell, D. *The Coming of Post-Industrial Society*. Basic Books, N.Y., 1973.

Berger, P.L. *Pyramids of Sacrifice*. Doubleday-Anchor, N.Y. 1976.

Birenbaum, A. & E. Sagarin. *Social Problems*. Scribners, N.Y., 1972.

Cherns, A. *Sociotechnics*. Malaby Press, 1976.

Gabor, D. *The Mature Society*. Praeger, N.Y., 1972.

Galbraith, K. *The New Industrial State*. New American Library, N.Y., 1985.

Huntington, S.P. *Political Order in Changing Societies*. Yale, N.H., 1968.

Little, D. and T. Gordon *Trends Likely to Affect Society*. Future, Middleton, 71.

Leiss, W. *The Limits to Satisfaction*. U of Toronto, 1976.

Lyotard, J-F. *The Post-Modern Coalition*. Minnesota U.P. Minneapolis, 1984

Martin, J. *Telematic Society*. Prentice-Hall, Englewood Cliffs, N.J., 1981.

Martin, J. *The Wired Society*. Prentice Hall, N.Y., 1978.

Marcson, S. (ed.) *Automation, Alienation & Anomie*. Harper & Row, N.Y., 1970.

Michael, D.N. *The Unprepared Society*. Harper-Colophon, N.Y., 1970.

Presthus, R. *The Organic Society*. St. Martin's, N.Y., 1978.

Silvertown, J. & Sarre, P. (Eds). *Environment & Society*. Open U., London, 1990

Thompson, E.S.W. *Sociocultural Systems*. Brown, Dubuque, 1977.

Valaskakis, K. et al. *The Conserver Society*. Harper-Colophon, N.Y. 1979

Technosociety

Communications

Alexandrowic, C.H. *The Law of Global Communications*. Columbia, N.Y., 1971.

Bordemare, J.E.D. *Communication & Rural Development*. UNESCO, Paris, 1977.

Cherry, C. *World Communication: Threat or Promise.* Wiley, N.Y., 1977.

Chisholm, D. (ed.) *Communications & Computers.* Science Council, Ottawa,'78.

Deutsch, K. *Nationalism and Social Communication.* MIT, Cambridge, 1953.

Fagan, R. *Politics and Communication.* Little Brown, Boston, 1966.

Frederich, H. H. *Global Communication & I.R.* .Wadsworth, Belmont, 1993

Gagnon, W. (ed.) *Nationalism, Technology & the Future* Macmillan, Toronto,1976.

Gerbner, G. (ed.) *Man, Media & Politics in Changing Cultures.* Wiley, N.Y., 1977.

Gerbner, G.*Communications Technology & Social Policy.* John Wiley, N.Y., 1973

Gerbner, G., et al. *Social Control Through Communications:* Wiley, N.Y., 1973.

Greenberg, M. *Computers, Communications & Public Interest.* Hopkins, Balt, 71

Hancock, A. *Communication Planning for Development* UNESCO, Paris 1981.

Harms, L.S. *Intercultural Communication.* Harper and Row, N.Y., 1973.

Hellman, H. *Communications in the World of the Future.* Evans, 1975.

Hiltz, S. and M. Turoff. *The Network Nation.* Addison-Wesley, Reading, 1978.

Krippendorff, K. (ed.) *Communication & Social Control* Gordon & Breach, N.Y., 79.

Kates, J. *Technological Sovereignty.* Science Council, Ottawa, 1977.

Lauden, K. *Communications Technology & Democratic Participation.* Praeger, 77.

Lee, J.A.R. *Towards Realistic Communication Policies.* UNESCO, Paris, 1976.

Meadow, R.G. *Politics as Communication.* Ablex, N.J., 1980.

Martin, J. *Future Developments in Telecommunications.* Prentice Hall, N.J, 77.

McBride, S. et.al. *Many Voices, One World.* UNESCO, Paris, 1980.

Merritt, R.L. (ed.) *Communication in International Politics.* Ill U.P., Urbana, 72.

Melody, W.H. et.al. *Culture, Communication & Dependency.* Ablex, N.J., 1980.

Nordernstreng, K. & H. Schiller. *National Sovereignty & International Communication.* Ablex, Norwood, N.J. 1979.

Niles, J.M. et.al. *Telecommunication-Transportation Tradeoff* Wiley, N.Y. 1976

Pool, I. (ed.) *Social Impact of the Telephone.* MIT, Cambridge, 1977.

— *Refocusing Government Communications Policy.* Aspen, Wash., 1976.

Porat, M.V. *Communications for Tomorrow.* Praeger, N.Y., 1978.

Pye, L. (ed.). *Communication & Political Development.* Princeton, N.J., 1963.

Prosner, M.H. (ed.) *Intercommunications Among Nations* Harper-Row, N.Y., 73.

Richstad, J.A. & L.S. Harms. *World Communication.* E-W Center, Honolulu, 73.

Schramm, W. *Big Media, Little Media.* Sage, Beverly Hills, 1977.

Schramm, W. & D. Lerner. *Communication & Change.* Hawaii, Honolulu, 1976.

Somerlad, E.L. *National Communication Systems.* UNESCO, Paris, 1975.

Teheranian, M. et al (eds.) *Communications Policy for National Development* Routledge & Kegan Paul., London, 1977.

Technology

Allen, T.J. *Managing the Flow of Technology.* MIT, Cambridge, 1977.

Armitage, W.H. *The Rise of the Technocrats*. Kegan Paul, London, 1965.

Basiuk, V. *Technology and World Politics*. Columbia, N.Y., 1977.

Baranson, J. *Technology and the Multinationals*. Lexington, Mass, 1978.

Boorstin, D.J. *The Republic of Technology*. Harper Row, N.Y., 1978.

Boyle, A. (ed.) *The Politics of Technology*. Open University., Cardin, 1977.

Burke, J.G. (ed.) *The New Technology & Human Values*. Wadsworth, Belm, 72.

Calder, N. *Technopolis*. Simon and Schuster (Clarion), N.Y., 1970.

Ellul, J. *The Technological Society*. Knopf, N.Y., 1965.

Drucker, P.F. *Technology, Management & Society*. Harper & Row, N.Y., 1970.

Ferkiss, V.C. *Technological Man*. NAL (Mentor), N.Y., 1969.

Fisher, F. *Technocracy & Politics*. Sage, Newbury Park, 1990

Gendron, B. *Technology and the Human Condition*. St. Martins, N.Y., 1977.

Gerstenfeld, A. (ed.) *Technological Innovation*. Wiley, N.Y., 1979.

Ginsberg, E. (ed.) *Technology and Social Change*. Columbia, N.Y., 1964

Granger, J.V. *Technology and International Relations*. Freeman, S.F., 1979.

Hetman, F. *Society and the Assessment of Technology*. OECD, Paris, 1973.

Hill, C.T. & J.M. Utterback (eds.) *Technological Innovation*. Pergamon, N.Y., 79.

Jantsch, E. *Technological Planning and Social Futures*. John Wiley, N.Y., 1972

McKinley, K. *Technology & the Third World*. North-South, Ottawa, 1979.

Mendes, C. (ed.) *The Controls of Technocracy*. Educam, Brazil, 1979.

Mesthene, M.G. *Technological Change*. Harvard, Cambridge, 1970.

Mitcham, C. & R. MacKay (eds.) *Philosophy & Technology*. Free Press, N.Y., 72.

Montgomery, J.D. *Technology & Civic Life*. M.I.T. Cambridge, 1974.

Nichols, K.G. *Technology on Trial*. OECD, Paris, 1979.

Nelkin, D. *Technological Decisions & Democracy*. Sage, London, 1977.

Ritterbush, R.C. (ed.) *Technology & Human Values*. Acropolis, Wash, 1974.

Schon, D. *Technology and Change*. Delta, N.Y., 1967.

Stover, C.F. (ed.) *The Technological Order*. Wayne State, Detroit, 1963.

Theobald, R.A. *Dialogue on Technology*. Bobbs-Merrill, Indianapolis, 1967.

Teich, A.H. (ed.) *Technology and Man's Future*. St. Martin's, N.Y., 1977.

Webster, B.R. *Technology & Access to Communications* UNESCO, Paris, 1975.

Williams, R. *Politics and Technology*. Macmillan, London, 1971.

Winner, L. *Autonomous Technology*. MIT, Cambridge, 1977.

Democracy

Barber, J.D. *Citizen Politics*. Chicago, Markham Pub., 1969.

Berrigan, F.J. (ed.) *Access: Western Models of Community Media*. UNESCO, 1977.

Bejold, D. (ed.) *Anticipatory Democracy*. Random House, N.Y., 1978.

Burns, T.R. *Creative Democracy*. Praeger, N.Y. 1988

Berger, P. & R. Neuhaus. *To Empower People*. AEIPPR, Washington, 1977.

Bendix, R. *Nation-Building & Citizenship*. John Willey, N.Y., 1974.

Bonello, C.G. (ed.) *Participatory Democracy*. Grossman, N.Y., 1971.

Clor, H. *Mass Media & Modern Democracy*. Rand McNally, Chicago, 1974.

Dahl, R. *Polyarchy*. Yale U.P. N.H. 1971

Dryzek, J.S. *Discursive Democracy*. Cambridge U.P. N.Y. 1990

Gould, C.C. *Rethinking Democracy*. Cambridge U.P. N.Y. 1988

Groombridge, B. *Television & Participation*. Council of Europe, Strasbourg, 73.

Illich, I. *Tools for Conviviality*. Harper and Row, N.Y., 1973.

Jenkins-Smith, H.C.*Democratic Politics & Policy Analysis*. Brooks/Cole,1990

Johansen, R. et.al. *Electronic Meetings*. Addison-Wesley, Reading, 1979.

Johnson, N. *How to Talk Back to Your Television Set*. Bantam, N.Y., 1970.

Kristov, S. *Representative Bureaucracy*. Prentice-Hall, N.J., 1974.

Lewis, P.M. *Whose Media?* (A Citizen's Guide). Cox & Wyman, London, 1978.

Manheim, J. *Can Democracy Survive Television?* Prentice-Hall, N.J., 1977.

Milbrath, L. *Political Participation*. Rand-MacNally, Chicago, 1965.

Pool, Ithiel de Sola. *Talking Back*. MIT Press, Cambridge, 1973.

Pranger, R.J. *The Eclipse of Citizenship*. Holt-Rinehart-Winston, 1968.

Saldich, A.R. *Electronic Democracy*. Praeger, N.Y., 1979.

Sewell, W. & J. Coppoct (eds.) *Public Participation Planning*. Wiley, London, 77.

Shepard, J.M. *Automation & Alienation*. MIT Press, Cambridge, Mass., 1971.

Schwoebel, J. *La Démocratisation de l'information*. UNESCO, Monograph#70.

Theobald, R. *Beyond Despair:* Seven Locks Press, Washington, D.C., 1981.

Valle, J. *Network Conferencing.* Datamation, May, 1974.

Politics

Arnopoulos, P.J. *Prospects for Peace.* Gamma Press, Montreal, 1986

Andrain, C.F. *Political Life & Social Change.* Wadsworth, Bel 1970.

Benjamin, R. *The Limits of Politics.* Chicago, 1980.

Butz, O. *Of Man & Politics.* Holt-Rinehart-Winston, N.Y. 1964.

Crick, B. *In defence of Politics.* Penguin, Middlesex, 1964.

Duverger, M. *The Idea of Politics.* Methuen, London, 1966.

Hoy, T. (ed.) *Politics & Power.* Capricorn, N.Y. 1968.

Iyer, R.N. *Parapolitics.* Oxford, N.Y. 1979.

Jouvenel, B. *Pure Theory of Politics.* Yale, N.H. 1962.

Kariel, H.S. *The Promise of Politics.* Prentice-Hall, N.J. 1966.

Konrad, G. *Antipolitics.* Harcourt, Brace, Jovanovich, N.Y. 1984

Lipset, S.M. *Political Man.* Anchor, N.Y. 1963.

Lasswell, H. *Politics: Who gets what, when & how.* Meridian, N.Y. 1958.

Laing, R.D. *The Politics of Experience.* Pantheon, N.Y. 1967.

Lindlom, C.E. *Politics and Markets.* Basic Books, N.Y., 1977.

Merriam, C. *Political Power.* Collier, N.Y. 1964.

Mackinnon, F. *Postures & Politics.* U of Toronto, 1973.

Parekh, B. and R. Berki (eds.) *The Morality of Politics.* Allen-Unwin, 1972.

Pennock, J.R. and J. W. Chapman (eds.), *Human Nature in Politics.* NYU, 1977.

Plano, J.C. and R. Riggs. *Dictionary of Political Analysis.* Dryden, N.Y 1973.

Rule, J. et.al. *The Politics of Privacy.* NAL (Mentor), N.Y., 1980.

Spiro, H.J. *Politics as the Master Science*. Harper-Row, N.Y. 1970.

Talmor, E. *Mind & Political Concepts*. Pergamon, N.Y. 1979.

Tinder, G. *Political Thinking*. Little-Brown, Boston, 1970.

Titmus, R.M. *Social Policy*. Allen, Unwin, London, 1974.

Waldman, S.R. *Foundations of Political Action*. Little, Brown, Boston, 1972.

Weinstein, M.A. (ed.) *Identity, Power & Change*. Scott-Foresman, Gl. 1971.

Development

Athorpe, R. *People, Planning & Development*. Frank Cass, London, 1970.

Appelbaum, R. *Theories of Social Change*. Markham, Chicago, 1970.

Black, C.E. *The Dynamics of Modernization*. Harper & Row, N.Y. 1967.

Bauer, P.T. *Dissent on Development*. Harvard, Cambridge, 1972.

Boulding, K.E. *A Primer on Social Dynamics*. Free Press, N.Y. 1970.

Clark, R.P. *Development & Instability*. Dryden, Hinsdale, 1974.

Etzioni, A. and E. (eds.) *Social Change*. Basic Books, N.Y. 1964.

Horowitz, I.L. *Three Worlds of Development*. Oxford, N.Y. 1966.

Holt, R.T. *The Politics of Economic Development*. Van Nostrand, 1966.

Lapier, R.T. *Social Change*. McGraw-Hill, N.Y. 1965.

Land, G.T.L. *Grow or Die*. Delta-Dell, N.Y. 1973.

Levy, M. *Modernization*. Basic Books, N.Y. 1972.

Lasswell, H. et.al. *Values & Development*. M.I.T., Cambridge, 1976.

Lippitt, G. *Visualizing Change*. University Associates, La Jola, 1973.

Meadows, P. *The Many Faces of Change*. Schenkman, Cambridge, 1971.

Moore, W.E. *Social Change*. Prentice-Hall, N.J. 1963.

Montagu, A. *The Direction of Human Development*. Hawthorn, N.Y. 1970.

Morse, C. et.al. *Modernization by Design*. Cornell, Ithaca, 1969.

Nisbet, R. *History of the Idea of Progress*. Basic Books, N.Y. 1979.

Nisbet, R. (ed.) *Social Change*. Harper-Torchbooks, N.Y. 1972.

Ogburn, W.F. *On Culture & Social Change*. Chicago U Press, 1964.

Oxaal, T. et.al. *Beyond the Sociology of Development*. London, 1975.

O'Toole, J. *Energy & Social Change*. M.I.T. Cambridge, 1976.

Parsons, T. *The Evolution of Societies*. Prentice-Hall, N.Y. 1977.

Pearson, L.B. *Partners in Development*. Praeger, N.Y., 1969.

Roxborough, I. *Theories of Underdevelopment*. Macmillan, London, 1979.

Schon, D.A. *Beyond the Stable State*. Norton, N.Y. 1971.

Schramm, W. *Mass Media & National Development*. Stanford, Palo Alto, 1964.

Shugarman, D.P. (ed.) *Thinking About Change*. U of Toronto, 1974.

So, A.Y. *Social Change & Development*. Sage, N.Y. 1990

Weiner, M. *Modernization*. Basic Books, N.Y. 1966.

Jensen, U. & R. Harre (eds) *Philosophy of Evolution*. Harvester Brighton, 1981.

Political Development

Adelman, I. and C. Morris. *Society, Politics & Development*. Hopkins, 1967.

Apter, D. *Political Change*. Cass, London, 1973.

Anderson, C.W. et.al. *Issues of Political Development.* Prentice-Hall, 1967.

Auster, R.D. & M. Silver. *Economic Forces in Political Development.* Martinus Nijhoff, Boston, 1979.

Benjamin, R.W. *Patterns of Political Development* McKay, N.Y., 1972.

Beer, S.H. *Modern Political Development.* Random House, N.Y., 1974.

Brewer, G.D. *Political Development & Change.* Free Press, N.Y., 1975.

Binder, L. et.al. *Crises in Political Development.* Princeton, N.J., 1971.

Braibanti, R. (ed.) *Political & Administrative Development.* Duke U, 1969.

Clifton, S. *Defining Political Development.* Lynne Riener, Boulder, 1988.

Coleman, J.S. (ed.) *Education & Political Development.* Princeton, 1965.

Dodd, C.H. *Political Development.* Macmillan, London, 1972.

Finkle, J.L. (ed.) *Political Development & Social Change.* Wiley, N.Y., 1966.

Higgins, E., D. Ruble, W. Hartup (eds.) *Social Development.* Cambridge, N.Y. '83.

Jaguaribe, H. *Political Development.* Harper & Row, N.Y. 1973.

Krishna. *Political Development.* Oxford, London, 1980.

Kohlberg, L. *Essays on Moral Development.* Harper & Row, S.F., 1981.

LaPalombara, J. *Bureaucracy & Political Development.* Princeton, 1963.

Merkl, P.E. *Political Continuity & Change.* Harper & Row, N.Y., 1969.

Organski, A.F.K. *Stages of Political Development.* Knopf, N.Y., 1965.

Palmer, M. and L. Stern (eds.).*Political Development.* Heath, Lex., 1971.

Palmer, M. *Dilemmas in Political Development.* Peacock, Ill., 1980.

Park, H.S. *Human Needs & Political Development*. Schenkman, Cambridge, 84.

Pye, L.W. *Aspects of Political Development*. Little-Brown, Boston, 1966.

Samuels, R. *Political Generations & Political Development*. Heath, 1977.

Shils, E. *Political Development in New States*. New York, 1964.

Tsurutani, T. *The Politics of National Development*. Chandler, N.Y., 1973.

Welch, C.E. (ed.) *Political Modernization*. Belmont, California, 1967.

Wilson, R.W. & G.J. Schochet. *Moral Development & Politics*. Praeger, 1979.

Weiner, M. & S. Huntington (eds.) *Understanding Political Development*. Harper-Collins, N.Y., 1987.

- Cap-Saint-Ignace
- Sainte-Marie (Beauce)
  Québec, Canada
  1995

«L'IMPRIMEUR»